Helena '98

FOOD
FROM YOUR
GARDEN

To my mother,
Jean Godbold,
for all her
support and inspiration

FOOD FROM YOUR GARDEN

Jennifer Godbold-Simpson

Principal photographer
Craig Fraser

Illustrations by
Darren McLean

STRUIK

Struik Publishers (Pty) Ltd
(a member of The Struik Publishing Group (Pty) Ltd)
Cornelis Struik House
80 McKenzie Street
Cape Town 8001

Reg. No.: 54/00965/07

First published in 1995

Copyright © 1995 in text Jennifer Godbold-Simpson
Copyright © 1995 in photography Struik Image Library:
Photographer: Craig Fraser with the exception of:
M. Alexander pp. 55, 86; S. Brandt pp. 77, 81, 92, 94, 98, 101 (bottom left), 108 (top), 109 (bottom left);
N. Carsen p. 31; N. Gardiner pp. 15, 27, 33, 42, 70, 73, 78, 87, 95, 101 (right); J. Lloyd p. 9;
A. Proust pp. cover (centre small), endpapers, 22, 30, 56, 57, 84, 99; W. R. Tarboton p. 29;
M. Turnbull p. 51 (bottom right);
Z. Wahl p. 63; K. Young p. 80
Copyright © 1995 in illustrations Struik Image Library:
Illustrator: Darren McLean with the exception of:
Erna Schoeman pp. 25, 26 and 28
Copyright © 1995 in published edition Struik Publishers

Editor: Glynne Williamson
Concept design: Petal Muller
Designer: Peter Bosman
Design assistant: Lellyn Creamer
Cover design: Peter Bosman
Illustrations: Darren McLean
Stylist: Shelley Street

Typesetting: Struik DTP
Reproduction: Hirt & Carter (Pty) Ltd, Cape Town
Printing and binding: Tien Wah Press (Pte.) Ltd, Singapore

All rights reserved. No part of this publication may be reproduced, stored in a retrieval system or transmitted, in any form or by any means, electronic, mechanical, photocopying, recording or otherwise, without the written permission of the copyright owner and publisher.

Also available in Afrikaans as *Kos uit die Tuin*

ISBN 1 86825 709 6

Acknowledgements

The author would like to thank the following people and companies for their assistance:

* Alphen Home Farm
* Andrea Benn
* Sheila Brandt
* Constantia Wholesale Nurseries
* Murray Joubert
* Malan Seuns Kwekery
* Mayford Seeds
* Donald Miller-Watt of Starke Ayres for supplying the Vegetable Sowing Chart
* Straathoff's Group (Pty) Ltd
* Starke Ayres Nursery
* Steenberg Farm
* Vereeniging Nursery
* Vergelegen Estate

CONTENTS

Introduction 6

What makes Plants Grow? 12

Pruning Methods 32

Plant them in Pots 36

Vegetables 40

The Fruitful Choice 78

Herbs 102

Freezing your Produce 112

Fruit and Vegetable Gardening Calendar 116

Vegetable Sowing Chart 120

Glossary 124

Index 126

Fresh, nutritious vegetables, straight from the garden.

INTRODUCTION

For the last forty to fifty years, home gardeners have tended to concentrate their energies on growing decorative plants. Flowering annuals, bulbs, perennials, roses and lawn areas have taken pride of place. The result has been that the once popular vegetable garden has been relegated to an unseen part of the garden, a small area with a few herbs or, like the fruit orchard, does not exist.

More recently, however, people from all walks of life have become interested in growing their own produce rather than having to buy from vendors or shops. There is no reason why anyone with the smallest piece of ground, or only space for a few containers, should not grow fresh food.

Freshly picked fruit and vegetables are more nutritious than those which have been stored, even for only a few days, and by growing them in your own garden, you will know if any chemicals, especially insecticides, have been used.

Another advantage of home-grown produce is that you need pick only as much as you require. Buying vegetables and fruit often requires buying in bunches, pockets or kilograms which can prove wasteful if you only want to use one or two pieces at a time. On the other hand, growing enough fruit for jam-making, for example, would be much cheaper than buying it.

In the home garden, you are also able to grow vegetables and fruit which are seldom, if ever, offered in supermarkets and fruit stalls, although they may be available at speciality shops.

A major reason for growing your own crops, however, is the spiralling cost of living. For very little cash outlay, you are able to grow a wide range of fruit, vegetables and herbs. It has been shown that by careful planning and the right choice of plants, you need only a very small area to produce a steady supply of vegetables virtually throughout the year.

The aim of this book is, therefore, to show you how to grow food crops successfully by explaining how plants grow, the easiest and most economical growing methods, the most important growing techniques and the way to control pests and diseases.

The book concentrates on fruit and vegetables which are economical to grow, are prolific bearers and have a number of different uses. Nothing could be nicer than eating your own home-made jam, stewed or bottled fruit, or taking a packet of home-grown frozen vegetables from the freezer, while a basket of home-grown vegetables also makes a welcome gift!

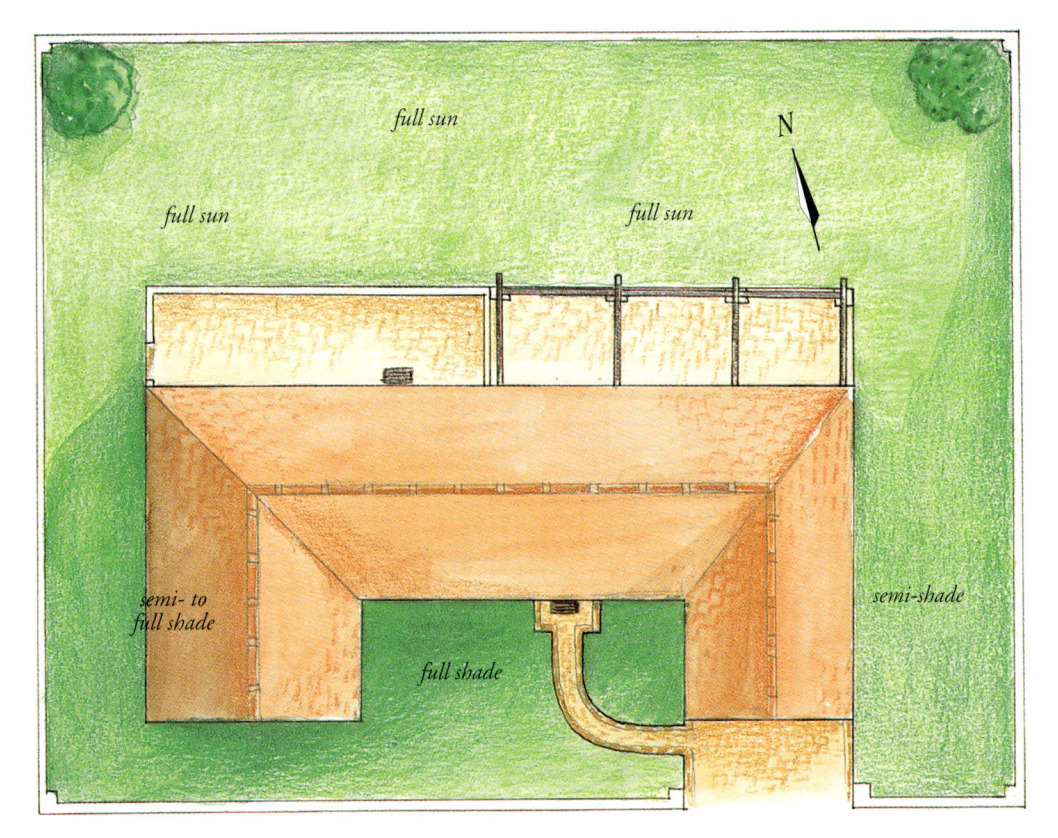

Basic garden plan showing the main features, as well as the areas of full sun, semi-shade and full shade.

PLANNING FOR SUCCESS

In order to grow a wide variety of edible crops successfully, first plan your garden carefully. Sketch your entire garden on a piece of paper. Depending on the size, use a scale of 1 cm = 1 m (1:100) for larger gardens, or 2 cm = 1 m (1:50) for small gardens and courtyards.

Draw in all the permanent and immovable features such as the house, garage or carport, driveway and pathways, patios and step areas, as well as large trees. Mark the position of drains and underground power lines. It will be useful, too, to find the north/south axis and the direction of strong winds. Lightly colour in the parts of the garden which receive full sun, morning shade, afternoon shade and those parts which are usually shaded throughout the day. The shade could be cast by your house, boundary walls and neighbouring buildings, or by trees.

It is crucial to establish the amount of shade an area gets as many plants, especially vegetables, do not thrive in insufficient direct sunlight. Remember that an area which is very shaded in winter may get more sun in summer, and vice versa. Once you have gathered all this information, it will be easier to establish the correct growing positions for the various plants. While in many ways it is easier to start a food-producing garden from scratch, even a fully established garden can gradually be redesigned to accommodate your crops.

Many people make the mistake of thinking that a garden which produces edible crops is purely functional and therefore visually unattractive. Provided you plan your garden well, it can always look attractive! The majority of fruit trees produce pretty blossoms as well as fruit, and provide as much shade and privacy as other types of trees. Use grapevines to cover pergolas, and grow other fruiting vines up fences or walls.

There are a number of fruit-bearing shrubs which can be grown in beds and borders along with different herbs. It is only the vegetable garden which can sometimes look rather regimented but even this can form an attractive part of your overall garden plan.

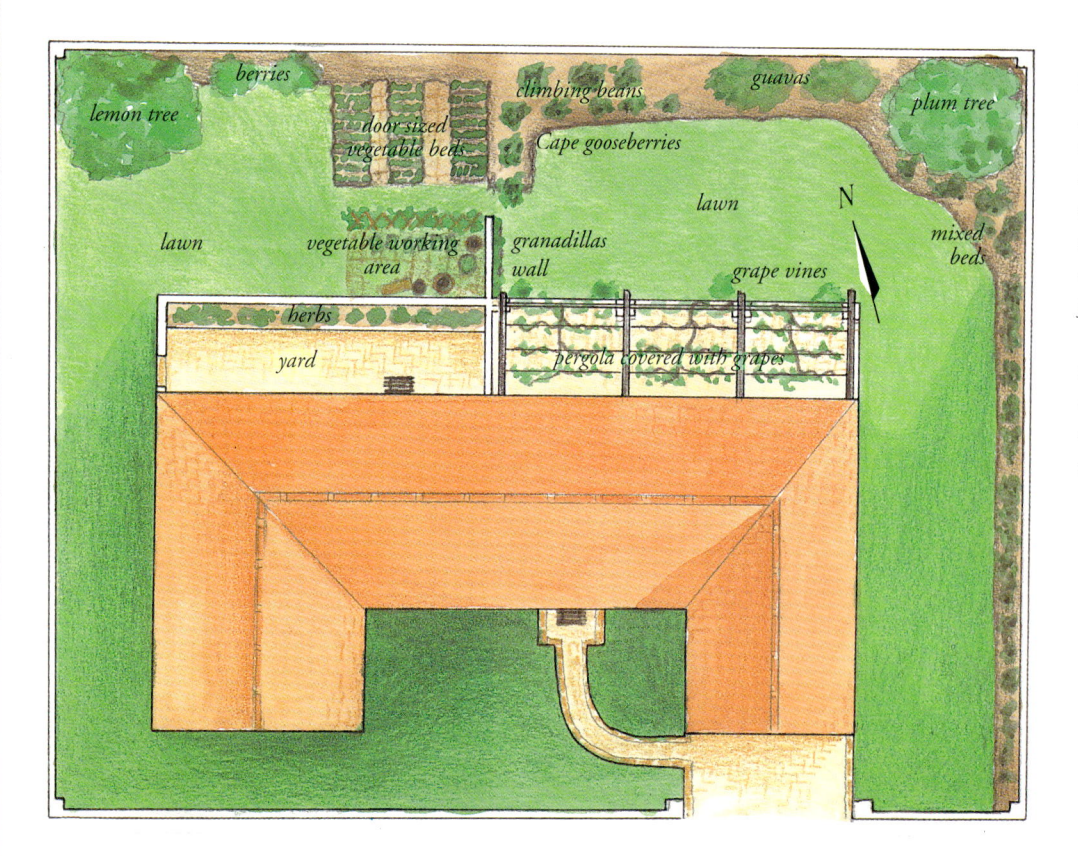

Deciduous fruit trees, such as apples, make excellent small garden trees.

Layout of a food-producing garden. The vegetable beds are sited so as to get the benefit of full sun. Climbers, such as granadillas and berries, are grown on fences and walls. The pergola is covered with grapevines, while a wall box in the yard is used for the cultivation of herbs.

INTRODUCTION

Functional but decorative: a garden with neat, boxed hedges around individual beds of vegetables and rows of standard roses.

WHERE TO PLANT VEGETABLES

When deciding on the best position for your vegetable garden, take the following points into consideration:
◆ Select a position which gets at least four hours of sun every day. Morning sun is preferable to afternoon sun which is harsher and may scorch the plants.
◆ Avoid planting vegetables right next to very large trees, hedges and shrubs which could cast too much shade and also compete with the vegetables for water and nutrients.
◆ Choose a spot which is protected from strong winds, especially cold spring winds and hot, dry summer winds.
◆ Be careful of frost pockets. Cold air sinks so frost is therefore more severe in low-lying spots.
◆ If possible, choose a level piece of ground. This makes watering and general care of your garden much easier.

The actual size and shape of the beds will depend on the available space and the type and quantity of vegetables you wish to grow (*see* page 44).

You may, however, find that you simply do not have a suitable growing area in your garden. This could be because the garden is very shaded or simply too small – you may live in a

Small, rectangular beds with narrow paths are easy to maintain and can contain a variety of plants.

9

town or cluster house complex with only paved areas. Don't let this stop you planning a vegetable garden! Many varieties can be grown in containers (*see* Plant them in Pots, page 37), providing they have a sunny position, but as containers absorb heat, it is better if the plants get some shade, preferably in the afternoon during the heat of summer.

Where to plant fruit trees

As any type of fruit tree will become a permanent and often large feature in the garden, its position must be chosen with great care.

◆ Make sure that it is planted in a sunny position with enough room for it to reach its full potential without overcrowding any other trees or plants.

◆ Do not plant a large-growing fruit tree too near to a building where it could be in the way of windows or doors.

◆ As blossoms on a fruit tree can be damaged by strong winds with a resultant poor fruit crop, the tree should be in a position where it is protected from very strong prevailing winds.

◆ In the colder parts of the country, a tree which could be affected by cold or frosty conditions should be planted in a warm, sheltered, north-facing position.

Fruit trees and garden design

In a larger garden, fruit trees can be planted to form part of the vegetable growing area. In smaller gardens, why not plant them in place of decorative trees, thus allowing for a number of different types?

Many fruit trees have attractive shapes and make excellent small shade trees. This is especially true of the various deciduous stone fruits such as peaches, almonds and persimmons. Be careful, however, that you have enough space before planting the really large-growing, wide-spreading types, such as figs, avocados, mangoes, litchis and pecans.

Citrus trees, with their handsome dark green foliage, sweet-scented flowers and colourful fruit, make ideal garden specimens, while cherry guavas, pineapple guavas, pomegranates and quinces make a welcome and attractive addition to a shrub border.

Where growing conditions are favourable, pawpaws and fruiting bananas make a dramatic feature. Consider, too, unusual softwooded fruiting shrubs such as tree tomatoes and Cape gooseberries.

Where to plant fruiting vines and creepers

In a food-producing garden, utilize as much space as possible by covering walls, fences and pergolas with fruiting vines and creepers. Like most fruiting

Rows of vegetables, shown against a backdrop of plum trees, provide the gardener with fresh produce.

Fruiting climbers are ideal for dividing up individual vegetable beds; a touch of mauve is added by low-growing thyme.

plants, they prefer full sun and protection from strong winds. In colder regions, many creepers do best when planted against a north-facing wall.

Of the fruiting creepers, pride of place goes to the grapevine. Vines make the perfect covering for a pergola. Being deciduous, they shade a stoep or patio in summer but allow in the sun during the winter months. Although they need a fair amount of care, your reward will be vines which are very productive.

The granadilla is a very vigorous and quick-growing creeper, ideal for covering wire fences or growing up a trellis against a wall. Unfortunately, it has a short life span and needs to be replaced every three to five years. As the plants grow easily from seed, you can grow new ones without much trouble.

If you need to enclose your vegetable garden with a fence to protect it from pets, if you want to divide or close off any part of the garden, or if you would like to cover an unsightly wall, then berries, such as the boysenberry, loganberry, youngberry and the newly introduced tayberry, are an excellent choice. Easy to grow in most parts of the country, they take up little actual space but produce heavy crops.

Herbs and companion plants

No food-producing garden would be complete without herbs. Widely used in cooking, herbs also have medicinal and cosmetic uses. Often more importantly, many of them are invaluable as companion plants, especially in the vegetable garden. Their unique properties can enhance the growth of other plants or act as pest and disease deterrents (*see* pages 103–106).

Where space allows, plant a special herb garden. Alternatively, herbs can be used as edging or bed dividers in the vegetable garden or can be grown amongst shrubs and other plants. Besides their many uses, a number of herbs have decorative foliage and attractive flowers, which is why they are such an integral part of the popular English cottage style of gardening. The leaves of various herbs, such as rosemary and mints, are also highly aromatic and give off a spicy or tangy perfume when crushed by hand or underfoot.

An array of summer vegetables show the various types which can be produced in a home garden.

WHAT MAKES PLANTS GROW?

While there are many factors which influence the growth of plants, two of the most important are the fertility and structure of the soil, and the prevailing climatic conditions. Gardeners can do a great deal about improving their soil by correct soil management, but to ensure that climatic conditions do not have a detrimental effect on crops, you need to choose types which are suited to your particular region.

CLIMATE AND PLANT GROWTH

Successful gardening depends largely on knowing your area's climate as well as the climatic requirements of your plants. This is of particular importance when growing vegetables as most have distinct growing seasons.

Frost is by far the most limiting climatic factor in South African gardening. The severity of the frost varies considerably from region to region and even within regions, depending on topography. In an area which experiences frost, this can be light on a north-facing slope but severe in low-lying and south-facing positions.

Rainfall and the availability of water are also very important factors. While permanent plants such as fruit trees, shrubs and vines can withstand periods of drought even if they do not produce good crops, vegetables, because they must grow quickly for the best results, cannot easily be grown under severe drought conditions.

Your local climatic conditions must therefore always be taken into account before you begin any planning. If you are unsure, it is wise to first consult a nurseryman in your area.

SOIL AND PLANT GROWTH

To grow successfully, plants must receive water, air and nutrients in the correct amounts for their specific needs. These essential requirements must be obtained from the soil in which they grow.

The most productive type of soil is dark brown in colour, crumbly in texture and is a mixture of clay, fairly coarse sand and decomposed organic material. A good soil, often called loam, will retain sufficient water and air for the plants' needs without becoming waterlogged or lacking in oxygen. It is also loose or friable enough for deep root penetration, but firm enough to support the plant. The mixture of mineral and organic particles in this type of soil contains enough nutrients for healthy plant growth.

Unfortunately, few unworked soils have all these ideal characteristics. Gardeners have to contend with a number of different soil types from light, sandy soils to heavy clay-based soils. The quality of soil can even vary considerably within the garden itself. All soils can be improved, however, by simple but regular soil management.

Before trying to improve your soil, you should understand what soil is and why soil structure is so important.

Well-drained, red, loamy soil

Black, 'cracking' soil

Well-drained loamy soil

Poorly drained, wet, clayey soil

Sandy top soil and clay sub-soil.

Food from your Garden

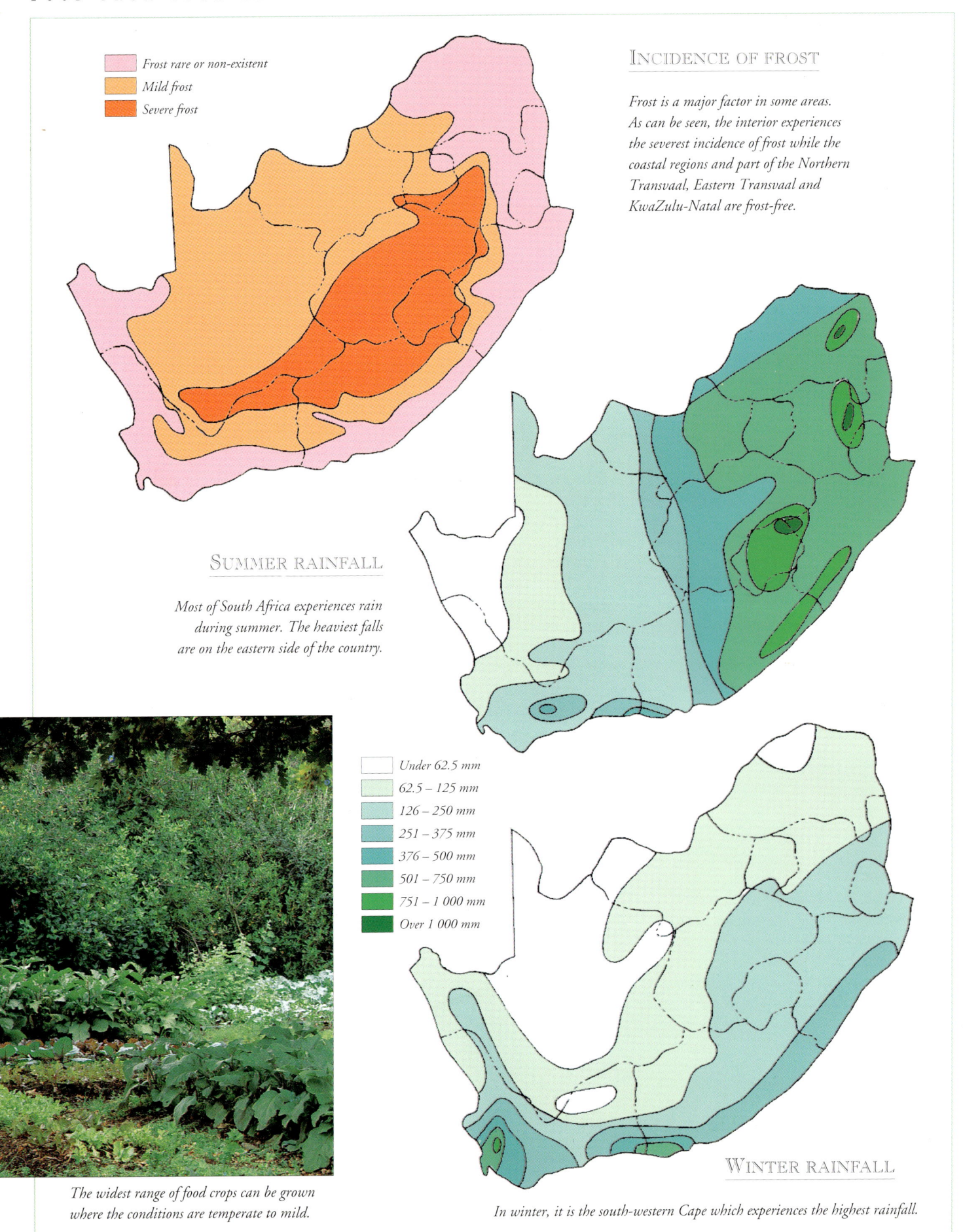

Frost rare or non-existent
Mild frost
Severe frost

Incidence of Frost

Frost is a major factor in some areas. As can be seen, the interior experiences the severest incidence of frost while the coastal regions and part of the Northern Transvaal, Eastern Transvaal and KwaZulu-Natal are frost-free.

Summer Rainfall

Most of South Africa experiences rain during summer. The heaviest falls are on the eastern side of the country.

Under 62.5 mm
62.5 – 125 mm
126 – 250 mm
251 – 375 mm
376 – 500 mm
501 – 750 mm
751 – 1 000 mm
Over 1 000 mm

The widest range of food crops can be grown where the conditions are temperate to mild.

Winter Rainfall

In winter, it is the south-western Cape which experiences the highest rainfall.

14

A healthy, well-structured soil is the key to success.

Soil basically consists of particles of minerals and organic (plant and animal) matter. While these may seem densely packed, they are surrounded by minute spaces, known as pore-spaces, through which the air and water move. Small organisms, especially various bacteria, mites and protozoa, which continue to break down the organic matter also live among the soil particles.

The actual size of the various particles classifies the soil type and whether it has a good or poor structure. Common soil types are clay, silty and sandy soils.

Clayey soils, for example, consist of fine, closely compacted particles. When wet, clay often becomes soggy but when dry it can become rock-hard. Because it is a compact soil, air and water move slowly through it. This type of soil is often low in plant nutrients and is difficult to work. Clay soils were often called heavy because, when cultivated with horse-drawn ploughs, a heavy team of plough horses had to be used.

Less compact than clay soils, silt is a fine-particled soil type which contains a fair amount of organic matter. Silt, which is relatively fertile, usually drains slowly and remains moist for long periods. There is poor air movement through silt, so plants could possibly suffer from a lack of oxygen.

On the other hand, sandy soils consist mostly of rounded grains of rock, especially quartz, which do not bind together easily. Because of their loose structure, sandy soils hold very little water and nutrients are rapidly leached out. Sandy soils are the most suitable for root vegetables but must be regularly supplied with organic matter.

While these are the main types, most soils are combinations of all three, depending on the proportion of the clay, silt and sand in each one.

The role of pH levels

While plants derive their growth nutrients from the soil, the ease with which they absorb and utilize the various nutrients depends to a large extent on the acid/alkaline balance of the soil. A scale of 0-14 is used to determine this important balance. Known as the pH scale, it measures the relative concentrations of hydrogen ions in the soil. A pH of 7 is said to be neutral. Levels below 7 range from slightly acid to extremely acid, while levels of above 7 range from slightly alkaline to extremely alkaline.

In extremely acid or alkaline soils, many vital nutrients cannot be absorbed and used by plants and this leads to nutrient deficiencies. Even adding the missing nutrient such as nitrogen or iron will not help unless the pH level is corrected at the same time. While the ideal pH levels for nutrient availability are different for each type of soil, most are fairly easily absorbed in soils which range between 5,5 and 7,5, with 6,5 being the best compromise.

How to improve your soil

The best way to improve your soil is by adding plenty of decomposed organic matter. Called humus, it improves the fertility and water retention of the soil. Dig it into the soil before planting, or mix it into planting holes with soil.

What kind of soil do you have?

Place a small quantity of garden soil in the palm of your hand. Add just a little water to make it soft, similar in consistency to plasticine or a soft dough.
◆ If it does not stain your fingers or stick together, and is gritty rather than silky and sticky, then it is a sandy soil.
◆ If it stains your fingers, binds together easily, and does not feel gritty but rather smooth, then it is a clay soil.
◆ If it does not stain your fingers and binds together readily but easily breaks into crumbs, then it is a good garden soil, referred to as garden loam.

Organic material can also be spread over the surface of the soil. This layer is then called a mulch. Besides improving the structure of your soil, mulching conserves water and regulates soil temperature. In time this mulch will decompose further and form part of the upper surface of the soil.

The easiest form of organic matter for gardeners to use is compost, which can either be bought or home-made (*see page 19*). Another form of organic matter is the rough layer of old leaves, known as leaf mould, which is found beneath trees and sometimes shrubs. You can also use peat moss, milled bark, spent hops, sugar waste, straw, decomposed sawdust, coir fibre and even shredded newspaper as compost.

Compost and other organic matter also play a vital role in improving the structure of the soil, allowing water and air to move freely and encouraging useful soil insects, earthworms and soil bacteria to live there. When added regularly and in fairly large quantities (about a wheelbarrowful per square metre of soil), well-made compost will improve the fertility of all soil types and help to correct extremes in pH levels.

Although it contains the three main major plant food elements (nitrogen, phosphorus and potassium) in small quantities, compost also contains virtually all the other vital elements. This means that well-composted soil has a natural balance of all the vital nutrient elements with each one reacting correctly with the other.

These nutrient elements (which include the trace elements iron, calcium, manganese, magnesium, sulphur, molybdenum, boron, copper and zinc) which all plants need in order to grow well are contained in varying amounts in the soil. As the plants grow, however, these elements are used up. Watering and heavy rains also leach out these vital elements.

Fertilizers are used to replace or add the missing elements and to improve the fertility of the soil. There are two main types of fertilizers, namely, the widely used artificial fertilizers, also called chemical fertilizers, and the increasingly popular organic products.

ARTIFICIAL FERTILIZERS

Artificial fertilizers are available in various forms. The most widely used by the home gardener is the balanced or compound granular type. Granular fertilizers are either worked into the soil prior to planting as a pre-planting fertilizer, or sprinkled and lightly dug into the soil around growing plants as a side-dressing. They always contain the three most important of the major plant elements: nitrogen (N), phosphate (P) and potassium (K), in varying amounts.

Different types of fertilizers are formulated for specific needs. One of the most suitable fertilizers for preparing vegetable beds and for feeding many types of vegetables is 2.3.2 (22). This contains 6,28% nitrogen, 9,44% phosphorus and 6,28% potassium. A well-balanced fertilizer, it has a fairly high amount of phosphorus as many local soils are deficient in this element. As fruit trees, fruiting shrubs, vines and creepers have different growth requirements, they should be fed with 3.1.5 (26). It contains 8,7% nitrogen, 2,9% phosphorus and 14,4% potassium. The higher amounts of nitrogen and potassium are needed for the development of a good stem structure, the formation of flowers and for fruit set. Used correctly, these fertilizers are one of the quickest ways to increase soil fertility. Other formulations are available, such as 2.3.4, 3.2.1 and 4.1.1. Fertilizers can either be quick-acting or have a slow-release nitrogen formula.

When a fertilizer contains only one element, it is generally referred to as a straight fertilizer. While many of the elements are available in straight form, the most important ones for the home garden are the nitrogenous types such as sulphate of ammonia (21% nitrogen), limestone ammonium nitrate (LAN) (28% nitrogen) and urea (46% nitrogen), and the phosphatic ones such as superphosphate (10,5% phosphorus) and basic slag (7% phosphorus). The most important thing to remember about granular artificial fertilizers is that

Alongside are three of the most widely used artificial fertilizers: 2.3.2 (22), 3.1.5 (26) and Superphosphate

Artificial Fertilizers

Type	Nitrogen	Phosphate	Potassium	Rate	Uses
2.3.2 (22)	6.3	9.4	6.3	50 to 125 g per m^2	general vegetables
2.3.2 (14)	4	6	4	50 to 75 g per m^2	general vegetables
2.3.4 (24)	5.3	8	10.7	75 to 125 g per m^2	general vegetables
3.1.5 (26)	8.7	2.9	14.4	60 g per m^2 or as directed	fruit trees, berries, etc
3.2.1 (28)	14	9.4	4.6	50 to 125 g per m^2	general vegetables
4.1.1 (33)	22	5.5	5.5	30 to 50 g per metre row	side-dressing vegetables
Ammonium sulphate	21	-	-	15 to 30 g per metre row	side-dressing vegetables
LAN (limestone ammonium nitrate)	28	-	-	15 to 30 g per metre row	side-dressing vegetables
Super-phosphate	10.5	-	-	100 to 500 g per m^2	pre-planting vegetables
				60 to 100 g per tree	pre-planting trees

they are strong and mainly quick-acting. You must always follow the directions carefully and never use them in excess – this can easily upset the nutrient balance of the soil and do more harm than good, especially when using the straight types. While granular artificial fertilizers will feed your plants, they do not improve the structure of the soil.

Apart from granular fertilizers, there are a number of concentrated types, either in liquid or powder form. These fertilizers are diluted with water and then either watered onto the soil around the plants or sprayed over the leaves as a foliar feed. You can get both balanced concentrates and straight ones. The balanced ones are particularly useful as they contain not only nitrogen, phosphorus and potassium, but also a range of the other elements, often called trace elements. While never needed in large quantities, trace elements play a vital part in plant nutrition.

Organic Fertilizers and Manures

The term 'organic fertilizers' can be somewhat misleading as people tend to equate them with the artificial types. Organic fertilizers, which are also called natural fertilizers, are made from the remains of living organisms. Before the advent of artificial fertilizers, these organic products were the only way to increase soil fertility.

Organic products, such as animal and poultry manures, contain virtually all the plant elements but in small and varying quantities. Dry cow manure, for example, contains the NPK equivalent of about 1.7:0.4:0.4, while poultry manure has an NPK equivalent of 2:1.2:0.6. Because of their high organic content and humus-forming properties, manures are also used to improve soil structure as well as soil fertility. Manures are usually spread in a thin layer over the surface of the ground and then dug into the soil when beds are being prepared for the various crops.

There are also a number of organic products available which supply plant elements: bone meal, which is an excellent source of phosphate and is used especially for trees and shrubs as a pre-planting fertilizer; hoof and horn meal, which contains a good percentage of nitrogen as well as small amounts of phosphorus and potassium; dried blood, which is high in nitrogen; and milled seaweed, which contains 2.88 N, 0.22 P and 2.29 K.

There are now also a number of organic soil conditioners and enriched composts available. These are often based on the by-products of industries such as the poultry, sugar and mushroom-farming industries.

Food from your Garden

On the whole, the dry organic products are slower acting than artificial fertilizers, but they remain in the soil for longer. The more bulky the organic product, the more it will improve the soil structure.

As well as dry organic products, there are a number of water soluble organic concentrates, including fish emulsion and seaweed concentrate. These also contain a wide range of plant nutrients and, depending on the product, various hormones and plant stimulants.

A hessian sack of fresh manure suspended in water makes an excellent liquid feed.

WHAT IS ORGANIC GARDENING?

For hundreds of years, mankind grew plants without the use of chemical fertilizers, pesticides and fungicides. Today there is a growing awareness of the importance of the environment and the dangers of pollution to air, water, animal life and food crops, as well as soil degradation, by the wide-scale use of chemical products.

Organic gardening is thus a method of gardening and growing crops using only organic products such as manures, composts and organic fertilizers to improve and retain soil fertility, natural substances to control pests and diseases, and growing insect repellent plants and companion plants, which for various reasons are beneficial to each other (*see* pages 103-104).

In many cases, where chemical products are too expensive or not available, gardeners are practising organic methods, perhaps unknowingly. While the successful growing of food crops by totally organic methods takes a long time to establish, you can certainly cut down your dependence on chemicals by making greater use of manures, composts, organic fertilizers and natural pest control methods.

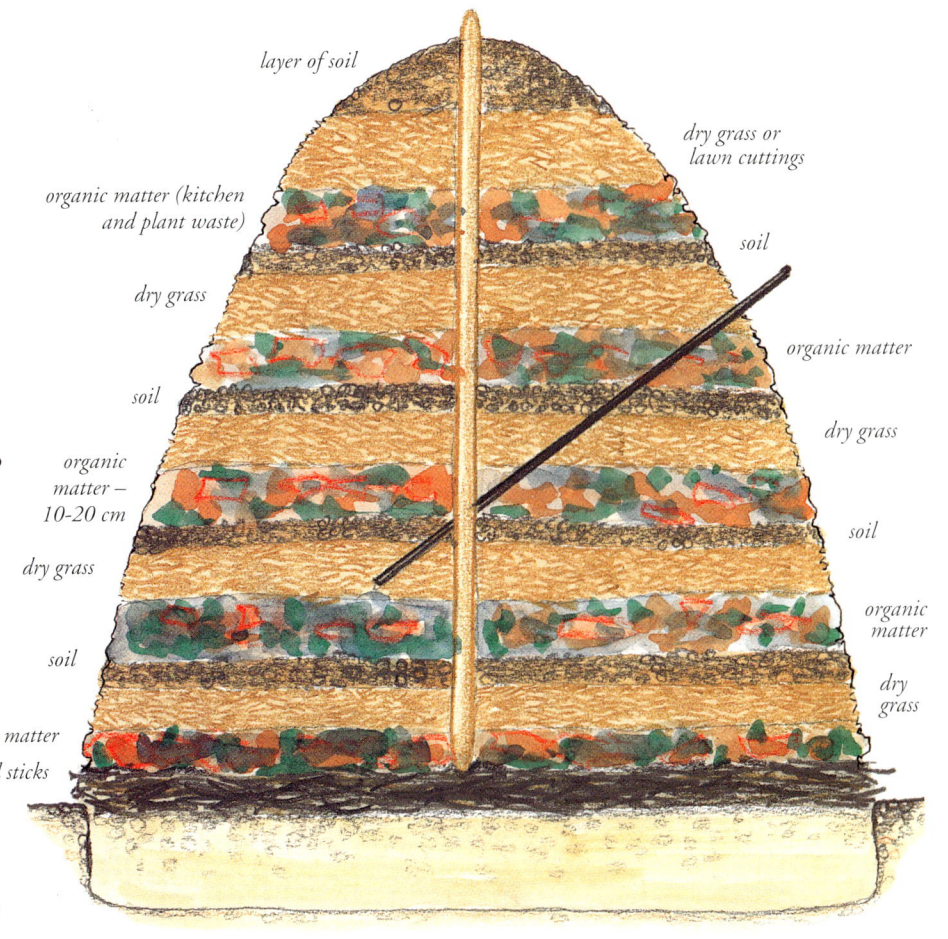

FERTILIZERS OR COMPOST?

A mistake which people often make is to assume that if they use artificial fertilizers, they do not need to use compost or any other organic material. Artificial fertilizers must always be used in conjunction with compost, otherwise the soil will deteriorate in its organic content with a resulting poor structure. However, regular use of bulky manures and other organic products will slowly but surely improve the fertility of the soil so that fewer artificial fertilizers need to be applied. Good quality food crops can be produced successfully without any artificial fertilizers and this is the basis of organic gardening.

Good compost is made by the careful building up of layers of kitchen and garden waste. Each layer is covered by a thin layer of soil.

HOW TO ...

To help with your gardening, I have included this section on basic gardening techniques, set out in a handy, concise way for easy reference while you plan, plant and care for your plants.

HOW TO MAKE COMPOST

While compost can readily be bought, most gardeners should be able to make enough of their own from their organic household waste and garden debris. It is vital to remember that compost is not simply a pile of rubbish – it needs to be made carefully for the best results.

There are a number of ways to make compost but the following method has been proven to be a reliable, easy and successful way:

◆ On a level, fairly sunny and open piece of ground, mark out an area about 1 m². Loosen the soil to about a spade's depth to allow free movement of bacteria and earthworms.
◆ Put down a 5-10 cm layer of small sticks and twigs.
◆ On top of the sticks put a 10-20 cm layer of plant and kitchen waste. Sprinkle it with a little animal manure if you have any. Water lightly.
◆ Cover the layer with 2-3 cm of soil.
◆ Continue to build up the heap layer by layer until it reaches about 1 m high. Seal the top and sides with a 5-10 cm layer of soil.

Your compost should be ready in about three months. Speed up the process by turning the heap.

HOW TO PREPARE VEGETABLE BEDS

As vegetables need well-worked soil, thorough initial preparation is worth the time and effort. One of the best ways to prepare vegetable beds for intensive cultivation in the home garden is to use the trench method, or deep bed method, in which soil and organic material are used so that they form a rich compost. It is a method used very successfully by many organizations to encourage vegetable growing in large urban and rural areas and forms part of the national Peace Garden concept.

◆ Mark out the size of your bed – 1 m x 2-3 m is a practical size.
◆ Dig the topsoil to a depth of about a spade and put this soil to one side.
◆ Dig out the subsoil to about 45 cm and put this on the other side. Remove all stones, builders' rubble and anything that will not decompose, as well as roots from surrounding trees.
◆ Put down a thick layer of organic material – kitchen waste, old plants, shredded newspaper, sawdust, anything that you would put on a compost heap – it does not have to be decomposed.
◆ Cover this with 10 cm of subsoil and water well.
◆ Continue to fill up the trench in this way until you reach ground level. Then take the topsoil, mix it with ready-made compost if possible, and make it into a mound on the top of the trench.

DO'S AND DON'TS OF COMPOST-MAKING

◆ Keep the heap damp but not saturated. The material should feel about as damp as a squeezed-out sponge.
◆ Try to mix waste material to get a good balance of wet or green and dry types.
◆ Do not put on thick layers of grass cuttings or thick layers of leaves as they form a mat and stop water and air reaching the rest of the heap.
◆ Large, coarse material such as cabbage and mealie stalks should be chopped up or shredded before being put on the heap.
◆ You can also make compost in an enclosure which has wooden, brick or concrete sides, as well as in a wire mesh cylinder or a plastic compost maker.

Because the top layer is soil, or a soil and compost mixture, you can plant and sow your vegetables directly into the trench. The lower layers of organic material will decompose gradually and you will have the ideal soil conditions for growing vegetables.

HOW TO PLANT TREES AND SHRUBS

Planting holes for trees, shrubs and other permanent plants must be well prepared. They should also be dug a month or two in advance if possible to allow the soil to settle. Never stint on the size of the holes. Trees need holes at least 45 cm wide and 45 cm deep. In very hard, rocky soil, try to make the holes up to 1 m² so that the plants can form plenty of roots before spreading into the hard ground.

◆ Dig out the topsoil and place it to one side.
◆ Dig out the subsoil and put on the other side.
◆ Loosen the soil at the bottom of the hole, put in a handful of superphosphate or bone meal and cover with a mixture of soil and compost.
◆ Place the plant in the hole to check the correct planting depth. The level of the soil around the plant should be the same or slightly lower than the surrounding soil but not higher. Put back some of the topsoil if necessary.
◆ Remove the plant from the plastic bag or take it out of its container. If the soil is dry, water first and allow to drain before you plant it.
◆ Set the plant in the hole, making sure it stands upright. If it needs staking, drive a suitable stake into the soil before you plant it.
◆ Fill the hole with the topsoil. Mix with equal amounts of compost if possible.
◆ Carefully tie the plant to its stake. Leave enough space so as not to strangle the trunk.
◆ Water well and then mulch with compost or a suitable material.
◆ Water regularly until established; if plants droop in very hot weather, spray the leaves as well.

FOOD FROM YOUR GARDEN

PLANTING VEGETABLE BEDS

1. Mark out the size of your bed according to the space available and to suit your requirements.

2. Dig out soil to about 45 cm deep. Put top soil to one side and sub-soil to the other. Put in pre-planting fertilizer and cover with a soil/compost mixture.

3. Fill up trench with layers of organic material and soil to ground level. Cover with top soil and compost.

PLANTING TREES

1. Dig a hole to the required size. Put top soil to one side and sub-soil to the other. Take out any stones, roots and other debris. Loosen soil at the bottom of the hole.

sub-soil   top soil

2. Put pre-planting fertilizer at the bottom of the hole and cover with soil/compost mixture.

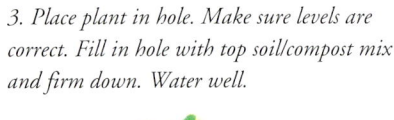

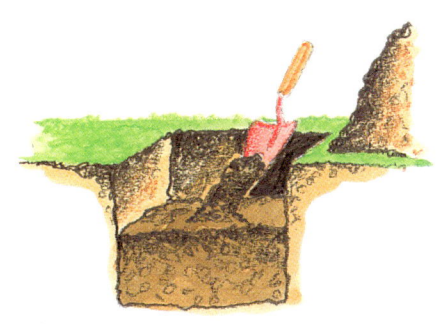

3. Place plant in hole. Make sure levels are correct. Fill in hole with top soil/compost mix and firm down. Water well.

HOW TO CHANGE pH LEVELS

The correct pH level is vital in plant nutrition and while good soil maintenance and the use of plenty of organic products and compost will usually help keep pH levels in the neutral zone, you may need to actively change your soil's pH level. Before doing this, first establish what the levels are. This can be done by testing the soil with a pH test kit or by using a pH meter.

If your soil tends to be very acid (below 5,5), you can raise the pH level by the careful application of agricultural lime. The amount you need to use will depend on the type of soil but usually ranges between 300-600 g per m². Heavy clay soils require more lime than sandy ones. Take expert local advice on how much lime, if any, you should apply. Remember, you can do great harm to your soil and your plants by using lime unnecessarily.

In the case of soils with a pH of above 7,5, gradually decrease the alkalinity by using 25-50 g of sulphur per m² or 60 g of ammonium sulphate per m². The use of plenty of acid-based composts and peat moss will also help to lower the alkalinity of the soil.

HOW TO APPLY GRANULAR FERTILIZERS TO NEW BEDS: PRE-PLANTING FERTILIZER

The active chemicals in an artificial fertilizer are contained in granules of an inert substance. To apply the fertilizer, measure out the required amount (i.e. 60 g per m²). Sprinkle it as evenly as possible over the surface of the soil. Take a fork or spade and work the fertilizer into the soil by turning the soil over. Rake it level and water thoroughly.

HOW TO APPLY GRANULAR FERTILIZERS TO GROWING PLANTS: SIDE-DRESSING FERTILIZER

Work out the amount of fertilizer you need for a particular crop, then carefully sprinkle the granules between the plants.

Very lightly work the fertilizer into the first few centimetres of soil around the plants, taking care not to disturb the roots. Water the plants and soil thoroughly, making sure that no fertilizer grains remain on the foliage as these could burn it. Never use more then the recommended rates.

How to apply granular fertilizers to trees

Measure out the required amount of fertilizer. Make a shallow, circular furrow just under the drip area (the imaginary line below the outer branches of the tree where the greater amount of rain drips down and where the tree's most active feeding roots are found) and place the fertilizer in the furrow.

Spread the fertilizer evenly in a narrow band under the drip area of the tree and work into the soil carefully.

How to use a liquid fertilizer or concentrate

Following the instructions carefully, measure the required quantity into a watering can. To make sure it mixes thoroughly, first dilute the fertilizer with a little water, shake it up well and then add the rest of the water. Soak the soil around the plants with the liquid. If using a liquid foliar feed, wet the leaves of the plants as well as the soil.

Roses, herbs and assorted vegetables make excellent companions.

21

How to add compost to the soil

To be effective, compost must be added in relatively large amounts, depending on the quality of the soil. When adding compost to planting beds, use about one wheelbarrowful of compost per m². Spread the compost over the top of the soil, then dig it into the top of the soil to about a spade's depth.

A thick mulch of compost keeps vegetables moist.

How to mulch

To mulch the soil around plants, put down a layer of any type of organic material. This can be compost, leaf mould, peat moss, milled bark, wood chips or any similar decomposed material. Before applying a mulch, however, water the soil well. Spread a layer about 10-20 cm deep over the soil. Avoid piling it against the stems of the plants.

How to raise vegetable seedlings

First find a suitable place to keep the seed boxes. This should be bright and airy but sheltered from harsh sun and protected from strong winds and heavy rain. The seed boxes can be special asbestos or plastic seed trays, cellular polystyrene trays, old seedling punnets or any other containers, provided that they have drainage holes. Magarine tubs and cream or yoghurt cartons can also be used. Fill with suitable soil. You can buy ready-mixed seedling soil or make your own. A good mix consists of two parts of garden soil, one part fine peat or sieved compost and one part coarse sand. Mix the ingredients well and sieve them if possible. Water the soil mix lightly. Fill the seed boxes or containers up to about 5 mm from the rim. Firm down the soil – use a suitably sized block of wood for large, flat surfaces – and then water with a fine spray.

◆ In large, flat seed trays, make shallow furrows about 5 mm deep and 5-7 mm apart. Sprinkle the seed as thinly as possible along the furrows and cover with a few centimetres of seedling mix.
◆ In smaller, flat trays simply scatter a small amount of seed on the surface and cover with soil.
◆ In cellular trays and small containers, drop in 1-3 seeds, depending on size, and cover with about 5 cm of soil.
◆ After covering with soil, water carefully with a very fine spray of water.
◆ Always keep the seed containers damp by watering frequently with a fine spray of water.
◆ If the seedlings come up thickly, thin them out to the approximate required number to give them more room to develop into strong, healthy plants. This can avoid the necessity of transplanting or 'pricking out' a second time.

How to transplant seedlings

Once the seedlings in their boxes or containers have developed into strong, sturdy, small plants (usually about eight to ten weeks after sowing, depending on the type), they must be transplanted into their growing positions, either into vegetable beds or containers in properly prepared soil.

◆ Dig small holes spaced correctly for the type of vegetable (*see* individual entries). The hole should be just big enough to accommodate the roots of the plants without disturbing the soil around them.
◆ Water the plants, then carefully take them out without breaking the roots or knocking off the soil.
◆ Place the seedlings in the hole, slightly deeper than they were in the seed box, gently firm the soil around each one and water gently.
◆ To stop the plants drying out too quickly, mulch lightly with fine compost, or lay dried grass or old leaves around them.
◆ To protect them from very hot sun until they are established, shade them with a frame of shade cloth, a wigwam of leafy twigs or even individual covers made from cardboard.
◆ To stop cutworms from eating young plants, work cutworm bait into the soil or use cardboard collars pushed into the ground around the plants to stop the cutworms getting to them. Protect seedlings from slugs and snails by using snail bait or a natural method.

How to sow vegetable seeds in a furrow

First break up the top 5-10 cm of the prepared soil by raking it backwards and forwards and taking out any rocks, stones or hard, lumpy bits of compost. This will make the soil fine and crumbly, giving it a good tilth. Make sure the surface is completely level.

◆ Mark out the required position of the vegetables in the bed by using a thin, straight piece of wood or a piece of string tied between two sticks.
◆ Make a shallow furrow along the length of the string or wood with a hoe or a stick. The depth of the furrow will depend on the type of vegetables you wish to sow.
◆ Scatter seeds evenly and thinly along the furrow according to their needs.
◆ Cover them gently with soil and firm the soil down with the back of a rake.
◆ Water lightly with a fine spray so as not to disturb or wash out the seeds.
◆ Keep the soil damp but not saturated until the seeds germinate.
◆ Use snail bait or other protection.
◆ If birds or cats are a problem, cover the soil with light wire netting or crisscross it with twigs and string.

WHAT MAKES PLANTS GROW

SOWING SEEDS IN A FURROW

1. Prepare the soil by breaking up lumps and raking it backwards and forwards to a fine tilth.

2. Mark out the area where the seed is to be sown.

3. Make a shallow furrow and scatter seeds along it.

4. Cover the seeds carefully with the back of a rake.

5. Water soil lightly but thoroughly.

TRANSPLANTING SEEDLINGS

1. Carefully take individual seedlings out of the tray.

2. Space correctly along row and make planting holes.

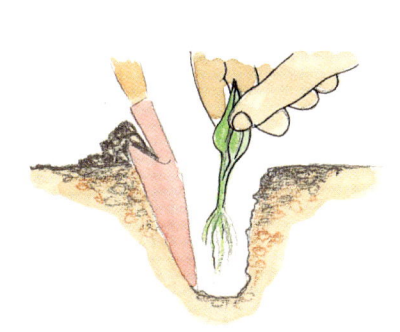

3. Place seedlings into holes.

4. Water in gently and cover with mulch.

SOWING SEEDS IN BOXES

1. Fill seed boxes with suitable soil and firm down.

2. Make shallow furrows across seed trays.

3. Sow seeds and cover with sieved soil.

4. When seedlings are big enough, transplant into boxes or into vegetable beds.

How to use water effectively

All plants, from young growing vegetables to established trees, must receive enough water. The amount needed will depend on the plant, the soil structure and the weather conditions. Quick-growing vegetable crops and plants in containers will obviously need watering more often than established trees and shrubs. On the whole, sandy soils will need more water more frequently than heavier clay-type soils. Rain will provide water but is frequently not enough or at the right time. You will therefore need to apply water for good crop results.

◆ Except for newly set out plants, do not simply sprinkle water lightly over the surface of the soil – allow water to stay in one place and to soak into the soil, about 15-25 cm at a time if possible.
◆ Use a watering system that waters the plants effectively. Do not waste water on unplanted areas or pathways.
◆ Consider putting in an irrigation system, which uses micro jets as well as drip irrigation.
◆ Make your own drip system by forming tiny holes along plastic or rubber pipes or hoses.
◆ Do not use sprinklers on windy days as this wastes water – rather surface irrigate by allowing the water to spread over the soil around the plants.
◆ Water in the late afternoon where possible, except in areas where mildew and other diseases are a problem. If this is the case, water early in the morning.
◆ To retain water in the soil, always use plenty of mulch.
◆ In very hot, dry conditions, vegetable seedlings will benefit from a midday sprinkling of water.

Take a 2 litre plastic cooldrink bottle and make three to five rows of small holes along the upper surface of it. Attach the hose to the top of the bottle and turn on the tap. The water will spray out like a sprinkler.

hand sprinkler

furrow irrigation

How to use waste water

Water that has been used in the household for various purposes can be re-used in the garden. The best waste water (also known as grey water) to use is bath or shower water as this has the least amount of soap.

You can also use the water from the last rinse cycle of your washing machine but always avoid using the water from a dishwasher as this contains heavy concentrations of harmful detergents. It is also better not to use the water from handwashing clothes because of the strong detergents.

Suitable waste water can be a life-saver when there are water restrictions, but using waste water at other times can help reduce your water costs.

Whenever possible, alternate waste water with fresh water as this will help to reduce the possible build-up of harmful salts and contaminants. You should also mulch the soil well with compost and other organic materials to help decompose any harmful build-up of salts and other residues.

How to control weeds

Weeds are simply any plants which are growing where they should not! Even pretty flowering annuals can be classed as weeds when growing in a vegetable garden. Weeds should be controlled as they compete with your edible plants for food and water, they can cause unwanted shade, and certain types are hosts for insects and various diseases.
◆ Regularly remove weeds from your vegetable beds and around your established plants.
◆ Pull out weeds while they are small – never allow weeds to go to seed.
◆ Careful hand-weeding among vegetables is the best method so as not to disturb the other plants.
◆ Heavy mulching will help in suppressing weeds.
◆ While selective weedkillers can be used on lawns and non-selective weedkillers on paved areas, there are as yet no weedkillers which are suitable for home garden use on vegetables and fruit.

Pests, Diseases and Disorders

While well-grown, well cared for plants are better able to withstand diseases and suffer less from insect damage and disorders than weak, underfed and under-watered plants, problems can still arise. It is vital to be able to identify what is wrong with a plant, understand the cause and know how to deal with it. Using insecticide on a plant which is suffering from a disease will not bring about the desired results and vice versa. It is also important to realise that many problems, especially if dealt with in the early stages, can be contolled without resorting to chemical measures.

CMR beetle

Ants

Fruit beetle

Cricket

A pest, disease or disorder?

A pest is a member of the animal kingdom which attacks plants in various ways. Nearly all the most troublesome pests are insects. Typical adult insects have six legs and range from tiny aphids to larger beetles and caterpillars.

Insect pests can basically be divided into two main groups: those which damage plants by making holes in foliage, flowers and fruit – the chewing insects – and those which suck out the vital plant juices – the sucking insects.

While the damage caused by the chewing insects is immediately obvious, that done by the various sucking insects can almost pass unnoticed. It is only when leaves and buds curl up and become distorted, develop lumps and bumps, or take on a silvery or bronze appearance, that the gardener realises there is a problem, by which time the pest has often disappeared.

Other insects which damage crops are stinging insects which lay their eggs on the fruit, for example, fruit fly. Many other creatures, while not insects in the true sense, are generally termed insects by gardeners. These include mites, woodlice, millipedes and the microscopic nematodes. Nematodes can become a serious pest in the garden. Snails and slugs are probably the most common and often the most destructive of garden pests. Moles can also cause havoc, especially in the vegetable beds. Even cats and birds if they damage your plants can be classed as pests!

A disease is a plant problem caused by a living organism which is spread from plant to plant. For diseases to develop, the organism must be present on the plant and the conditions for its growth favourable. Unlike pests, you cannot see the disease-causing organisms, only the symptoms. The majority of diseases which occur in the garden are caused by fungi, but bacterial and viral diseases can sometimes be a problem.

A disorder is also a plant problem which, while it might have disease-like symptoms, is not caused by a living organism. A lack of nutrition and poor soil structure are two main reasons why plants suffer from disorders. Environmental conditions such as wind and cold, as well as incorrect plant choice, all play a part. Pollution of air and water may often cause disorders.

Pests

American bollworm
A very destructive chewing insect, it feeds on the flowers and fruit of many vegetables, fruit trees, berries and vines.
Control: Hand-pick; use suitable herbal spray; use insecticide formulated for chewing insects.

Aphids
A tiny but prolific sucking insect, it is mainly green or black but also grey. It feeds on the young shoots of a wide range of plants and on the undersides of leaves and reproduces rapidly.
Control: Water off plants with a strong jet of water; use a soap or herbal spray or an insecticide formulated especially for sucking insects.

Astylus beetle
A pollen-feeding chewing insect, it can be a serious pest on strawberries.
Control: Hand-pick if possible; use a herbal spray or insecticide formulated for chewing insects; take note of withholding period.

Food from your Garden

Lawn caterpillar	White fly	Psylla
White grub	Aphid	Red spider mite
Cutworm	Australian bug	Pernicious scale
Fruit fly	Mealy bug	Chafer beetle

Australian bug
This bug can be found on fruit and vegetables but is not common and does not do much damage.

CMR beetle
A flower-eating chewing insect, it can be a serious problem on beans.
Control: Hand-pick if possible; use a herbal spray or an insecticide formulated for chewing insects.

Cutworm
A worm-like grub, usually grey, it lives in the soil and chews stems of newly planted seedlings at or just below ground level.
Control: Push cardboard collars into the soil around the plants; mulch plants with oak leaves; use a specially formulated cutworm bait.

Diamond-back moth caterpillar
A small, light green caterpillar, it feeds on the undersides of leaves, especially cabbages and other brassicas.
Control: Hand-pick if possible; use a herbal spray or an insecticide formulated for chewing insects.

Fruit fly
The adult fly lays eggs on the skin of fruit. After the maggots hatch, they burrow into the fruit, causing rotting.
Control: Pick up fallen fruit, soak in water for a couple of hours to kill maggots, then bury the fruit; make a bait of 500 g sugar and 15 g of suitable insecticide diluted in 5 litres of water. Hang jars filled with bait from the branches of the trees or splash onto the foliage. Bait the trees from the time fruit forms; use a chemical fruit fly spray.

Greater cabbage moth caterpillar
A green caterpillar, it feeds mainly on brassicas. Mature ones may have a white line and black spots along the back.
Control: Plant suitable companion plants; hand-pick large ones if possible; use a herbal spray or an insecticide formulated for chewing insects.

Green shield bugs
Also known as tip wilters or vegetable bugs, they are green to greenish-brown shield-shaped insects which suck the sap from a number of plants, especially beans and granadillas.
Control: Hand-pick if possible; dislodge with a strong jet of water, especially on the undersides of leaves; use a herbal spray or a suitable insecticide formulated for the insect; take note of withholding period.

Mealie bug
This bug can be found on fruit and vegetables but is not common and does not do much damage.

Pear slug
A black, slimy slug which feeds on the upper surfaces of stone fruits, especially plums, and can totally defoliate the tree.
Control: Spray with a herbal spray or use a suitable insecticide formulated for chewing insects.

Pernicious scale
A grey-black circular scale insect which sucks the sap from branches and twigs, especially deciduous fruit trees.
Control: Spray dormant trees in winter with lime sulphur; use a suitable insecticide formulated for scale insects.

Controlling ants in the vicinity of the trees also helps to stop the spread of pernicious scale from tree to tree. Badly affected branches should be removed immediately and burnt.

Plusia looper caterpillar
This is a green caterpillar with pale green stripes which chews the undersides of leaves, often leaving only a skeleton. It is especially destructive on beans, brassicas and tomatoes.
Control: Hand-pick large ones if possible; use a herbal spray or suitable insecticide for chewing insects.

Easy-to-make cardboard or plastic collars protect these young cabbages from cutworm.

Red spider mite
A minute mite, almost invisible to the naked eye, which sucks plant sap from the undersides of leaves. It causes leaves to go yellow or bronze and then fall off.
Control: Increase humidity around plants by spraying undersides of leaves during hot dry conditions; use a suitable systemic insecticide formulated for sucking insects.

Scale
See Pernicious Scale.

Slugs and snails
These are slimy molluscs which feed mainly at night on the leaves of young seedlings and mature plants. Slugs have no shells. Snails are large with brownish shells or small with white conical shells.
Control: Hand-pick; use attractants, for example, cabbage leaves, saucers of beer or up-turned black plastic seed punnets; use a specially formulated snail bait or a snail-killing liquid.

Stink bugs (twig wilters)
Large brown to black insects, stink bugs are very troublesome in some areas. They suck out sap from growth tips and flower stems, which then wilt, and are especially troublesome on granadillas, beans, eggplants and grapevines.
Control: Pick by hand if possible; spray with herbal spray or use a suitable insecticide formulated for the pest (adults hard to eradicate with insecticide).

Thrips
These are tiny, almost invisible insects which feed on plant sap. Usually only the damage is seen – silvery streaks appear on leaves. They attack many kinds of fruit and vegetables.
Control: Use a herbal spray or use a suitable insecticide formulated for sucking insects.

White fly
A tiny sap-feeding, waxy, white flying insect, similar to an aphid, it is troublesome on tomatoes and beans. It is very prolific and difficult to eradicate.
Control: Dislodge with a strong jet of water; spray with a soap solution; use a herbal spray or a suitable insecticide formulated for the pest; take note of withholding period.

FUNGAL DISEASES

Alternaria (early blight)
Dark brown or black spots with yellow rings develop on leaves. Older foliage is affected first. It can cause serious problem on tomatoes and potatoes.
Control: Only water plants early in the morning to ensure foliage is dry by nightfall, or surface irrigate; do not plant tomatoes and potatoes in the same beds season after season; spray with a herbal spray made from 2 cloves of garlic and 4 large onions boiled in 5 litres of water; use a suitable fungicide as a preventative measure – disease hard to cure once plants infected.

Anthracnose
This causes sunken spots on pods, fruits and leaves of many vegetables, especially beans and tomatoes, and fruit such as avocados, grapes and guavas.
Control: Avoid splashing foliage of plants with water; lift lower foliage off the ground or cut away; use a suitable fungicide as a preventative measure.

Damping off
This is a fungal disease which causes seedlings to rot at soil level.
Control: Use seed which has been treated with fungicide, or dust seed with suitable fungicide powder; sow seed as

Black spot

Downy mildew

Leaf curl

Early and late blight

Powdery mildew

Rust

BENEFICIAL INSECTS

While many insects damage plants, there are others which are counted as the gardener's friends because they feed on destructive pests. Birds, especially wagtails, white-eyes, swallows, swifts and shrikes, and chameleons both consume large numbers of insects. All the beneficial insects and pest predators should be encouraged and protected in the garden. It is important to remember that bees are also beneficial as they aid in pollination, an important factor when growing fruit trees.

Consuming vast quantities of insects, especially aphids, white eyes are among the gardener's best friends.

thinly as possible – thin out seedlings to prevent overcrowding; spray infected seedlings with a suitable fungicide. When sowing in seed boxes, use a sterilized seed-sowing soil.

Downy mildew
This causes pale green spots on upper foliage surfaces and white mildew on the undersides of many brassicas, yellow-brown spots on the under surfaces of peas, and pale yellow, oily spots on the upper surfaces of grape leaves with white, downy growth on undersides.
Control: Make sure plants are not overcrowded – need good air circulation; keep foliage as dry as possible – surface irrigate if necessary; spray with suitable fungicide.

Late blight
Watery spots develop on the leaves of tomatoes and potatoes, which then rot and fall off.
Control: Plant potatoes, tubers and tomato cultivars which are resistant to the disease; keep foliage as dry as possible, especially during humid conditions – surface irrigate; keep foliage off the soil; spray plants with a garlic solution as for alternaria; spray plants with a suitable fungicide formulated for the disease as a preventative measure – the disease is hard to eradicate once the plants are even mildly infected.

Powdery mildew
White, powdery deposit forms on the leaves and young stems of many vegetables and fruit trees, especially the stone fruits, as well as peas, peppers, tomatoes, courgettes and cucumbers.
Control: As for *Downy mildew*.

Rust
Yellow patches develop on upper surfaces of leaves and fine reddish spores form on undersides. It affects many plants, espcially broad beans, beans, apricots, peaches and plums.
Control: Do not overcrowd vegetables and avoid planting susceptible crops, for example, peas, in the same soil; surface irrigate to stop spores from spreading; always pick up infected leaves and destroy; spray with suitable fungicide formulated for the disease as a preventative measure.

How to avoid problems

◆ Always grow the right plants for your region's climatic conditions, plant them in the correct position and, in the case of vegetables, in the correct season.
◆ Try to buy the best quality seed possible and choose varieties and cultivars which have been especially bred for disease resistance.
◆ Do not plant out weak plants or those which show any sign of pests or disease.
◆ Do not grow the same vegetable crop in the same place season after season.
◆ Do not overcrowd plants – this encourages the spread of diseases.
◆ Plant a wide selection of plants to discourage specific pests multiplying on one variety.
◆ Grow plants with insect repellent properties, especially among vegetables.
◆ Encourage natural pest controllers such as birds, frogs, lizards, chameleons and predator insects which live off pests and consume large quantities.
◆ Keep a close watch on your plants and take action at the first sign of damage.
◆ Hand-pick larger insects and snails; use a strong jet of water on both the top and undersides of leaves to discourage aphids and red spider mite in particular.
◆ Remove weeds – they rob plants of food, water, light and space and can harbour pests and diseases.
◆ Do not leave rubbish lying around – it can become the breeding ground for insects and pests, e.g. snails and slugs.
◆ If a plant is 'sick' and doesn't respond to treatment, remove it before the problem spreads to other plants
◆ Only use chemical insecticides as a last resort and only on the plants affected; chemical fungicides, however, may be needed as a preventative measure on certain susceptible plants.

Beneficial insects

Hover flies
Yellow and black flying insects lay their eggs amongst colonies of aphids. When these eggs hatch, the larvae then feed on the aphids.

Lacewings
Delicate looking insects, mainly green and brown, they eat aphids and the larvae of mealy bugs.

Ladybirds
There are a number of different types of beneficial ladybirds or ladybird beetles. They usually have the typical red and black markings although there are also plain black ones. Both adult ladybirds and their prickly larvae feed on aphids as well as scale insects, mealy bug and Australian bugs. Keeping ants under control encourages ladybirds as ants are their main enemies.

Praying mantis
This odd looking insect with its long legs eats a wide variety of harmful pests, including aphids and grasshoppers. The female deposits her eggs in a white egg sac which is attached to the plant stem. When the baby mantises hatch out, they immediately begin feeding on the aphids.

Spiders
All spiders eat insects and so are beneficial in helping keep down populations of insect pests.

Wasps
While not thought of as beneficial, wasps play an important role in pest control. The adult wasp paralyses various types of larger insects, including beetles and caterpillars, leaving them next to their nests as a food source for their young. Certain wasps actually lay their eggs in the paralysed or dead insects so that food is at hand after the eggs have hatched.

Other beneficial insects include dung beetles, robber flies, dragonflies, assassin bugs, ant-lions, various ground beetles and flies. The insect pests are either eaten by the adults or used as a food source for larvae.

Using chemical products

If used correctly, chemical products, such as insecticides and fungicides, can help you to produce good crops of vegetables and fruit. They must be chosen extremely carefully, however, and only be used as directed.

When choosing a chemical product, first ensure that it has been formulated for use on edible crops and is not just for use on ornamental plants. Check that it can be used on your specific crop and take careful note of the withholding period. This indicates how many days must elapse after the last application of the spray before you can harvest and eat the crop (see Glossary).

Natural pest controllers, a chameleon waits patiently for its insect prey.

Watching for insects, the praying mantis helps control aphids and small grasshoppers in the garden.

Snails and slugs can be gathered by hand but an easier method is to put out cabbage leaves and then collect the snails which have gathered on them. Snails and slugs love damp, dark places and will also congregate under an upside-down seedling tray.

Using natural methods, such as non-toxic herbal sprays or growing companion plants (*see* pages 103-104), can also help to control various problems. You can also make your own sprays to help combat various problems.

Home-made sprays

Soap spray
Add a teaspoon of oil-based soap, such as green bar soap, to a litre of water and spray plants. Try to avoid using soaps or liquids which contain detergents as these can damage the plants.

Garlic spray for aphids, snails, caterpillars and cabbage moths
3 large heads garlic (about 85 g)
6 tbsp medicinal paraffin oil
1 tbsp grated oil-based soap (not detergent)
500 ml hot water

Roughly chop the garlic, put into a blender with the paraffin oil and pulverise, or rub through a grater. Scrape pulp into a bowl, cover and leave for 48 hours.

Stir grated soap into the hot water until melted. Stir soap and water into the garlic mixture.

When cool, strain into screw top jars and refrigerate. Spray the plants with 2 tablespoons of garlic solution to 2 litres of water.

Herbal spray for aphids and other pests
1 handful wormwood
1 handful rue
1 handful tansy
250 ml pure soap powder
2 litres boiled water

Boil herbs in a small amount of water for 5 minutes. Add herb mixture and soap powder to the 2 litres of boiled water. Strain and use to spray plants.

Do's and don'ts of chemical products

- Keep chemicals out of the reach of children and pets.
- Wash hands well after application in case of accidental skin contact.
- Always keep bottles and containers clearly marked.
- Always keep the leaflets found inside the containers as these have the full instructions – not all the information is on the bottle or box.
- Don't make the solution any stronger than directed.
- Don't mix sprays in a confined area – fumes can be very dangerous.
- Don't let any part of your body come into contact with the chemical – wear gloves and protective clothing.
- Don't spray under windy conditions.
- Don't eat or drink while spraying a chemical.
- Don't store chemicals near food.
- Don't ever decant a chemical into another container.

Other control measures

Many pests, while not totally eradicated, can be kept under control by other control measures. One of the simplest way is to hand-pick the pests off the plants. The larger insects, such as beetles and caterpillars, are easy to catch and must be destroyed immediately after being caught by dropping them into a water and paraffin mixture or an appropriate insecticide solution. The best time to catch these insects is at night or early in the morning.

Many of the smaller insects can be dislodged by spraying them with a hard jet of water. Spray both the tops of the leaves as well as the undersides. Stop cutworm damage to young seedlings by putting a paper collar around the newly planted seedling and pushing this into the ground. A thick mulch of oak leaves will also keep cutworms at bay.

This heavy-bearing pear tree shows the tiered system of branch development, as a result of using the central leader pruning method.

PRUNING METHODS

Fruit trees and vines need to be pruned on a regular basis to encourage them to produce plenty of flowers and then fruit. The amount of cutting back to be done will depend on the type of fruit. Citrus trees, for example, need very little pruning but the stone fruits, such as peaches and apricots, as well as vines, apples and pears, require a regular pruning programme to keep them in production.

The main aim of pruning is to encourage the production of new fruiting wood which will bear regular crops of quality fruit. Correct pruning will also allow in enough sunlight to ripen the fruit and will remove weak, diseased or damaged branches.

Young trees are initially pruned to achieve the desired shape and the annual pruning thereafter keeps the tree within that framework. Deciduous fruit trees and vines are pruned mainly in winter and evergreens in spring or autumn, depending on their fruiting pattern. Fruit and nut trees can be pruned to a number of different shapes, but the most common ones are the vase shape, the pyramid or central leader, and the modified natural shape.

VASE SHAPE

The aim in pruning to a vase shape is to keep the centre of the tree reasonably open and to encourage the upward and outward growth of the tree. The tree must be pruned fairly hard during the first few years to develop the correct framework. Once this has been achieved, annual pruning consists of maintaining the shape and removing branches which cross the centre or grow up into the centre. Very strong growing trees, such as apricots, may need to be lopped back if they get too tall. This system is widely used for peaches, figs, plums, apricots, apples and pears.

CENTRAL LEADER METHOD

This is an easy pruning method, well suited to a large range of both deciduous and evergreen fruit and nut trees such as guavas and macadamias, as well as apples, pears and all the stone fruits. The central stem or leader is allowed to develop and is not cut back. Side branches are trained to form a series of tiers with about four branches to each tier and 50 cm between the tiers.

As the tree grows it will form a pyramid shape. The aim is to produce a tree which is wider at the base and pruning is done by lightly shortening the side branches. The central leader method produces a very strong and attractively shaped tree but sometimes excessive shadiness in the centre can lead to a lack of fruit in certain types of trees, such as peaches. If this happens, some branches should be removed.

Correct pruning produces well-shaped trees and heavy crops.

Food from your Garden

Modified natural shape

Many fruit and nut trees, especially the evergreens like citrus and other very large-growing subtropical types, require little or no pruning as they will naturally develop a good shape and produce fruiting growth. Pruning consists mainly of removing any dead, damaged or diseased branches. The height of the tree can be contained to a certain extent by shortening the central leader and any very tall-growing side shoots.

How to prune vines over a pergola

The secret to producing successful grape crops from vines grown over a pergola depends on the initial training and pruning. This must be done with great care and carried out at the correct time of the year to achieve the desired framework. The vines will probably not produce grapes for the first three to four seasons but subsequently you will get good crops from easy-to-prune plants.

1. During the first winter after planting, cut back all the side shoots which have developed, leaving just the one strong main stem. Tie this carefully but firmly to the pergola support.
2. In spring, as the side shoots begin to grow again, cut back all of them except the strongest one at the top, which will then become the main stem.
3. Keep the main stem tied to the support and encourage a strong, straight stem by cutting off all the side shoots. Once it reaches the top of the pergola, tie it down firmly but allow the side shoots to grow out.

Careful and regular pruning will result in healthy, long-living trees.

4. In the second winter, cut back the main stem and any well-developed side shoots to pencil-thickness.
5. In spring, thin out the side shoots so that you have strong stems about 15 cm apart along the main stem. This is now your main framework.
6. Each winter cut back the shoots which developed during the summer months and bore fruit. Cut back as far as the last two shoots. Extend the framework of the vine over the pergola by allowing strong, new, secondary stems to develop away from the main trunk every metre.

Summer pruning

Certain deciduous fruit trees, especially apricots and some varieties of peaches, grow very vigorously. These trees benefit from being pruned in summer after their fruit has been harvested. This summer pruning consists of shortening back the long, fruit-bearing stems by approximately 30 cm.

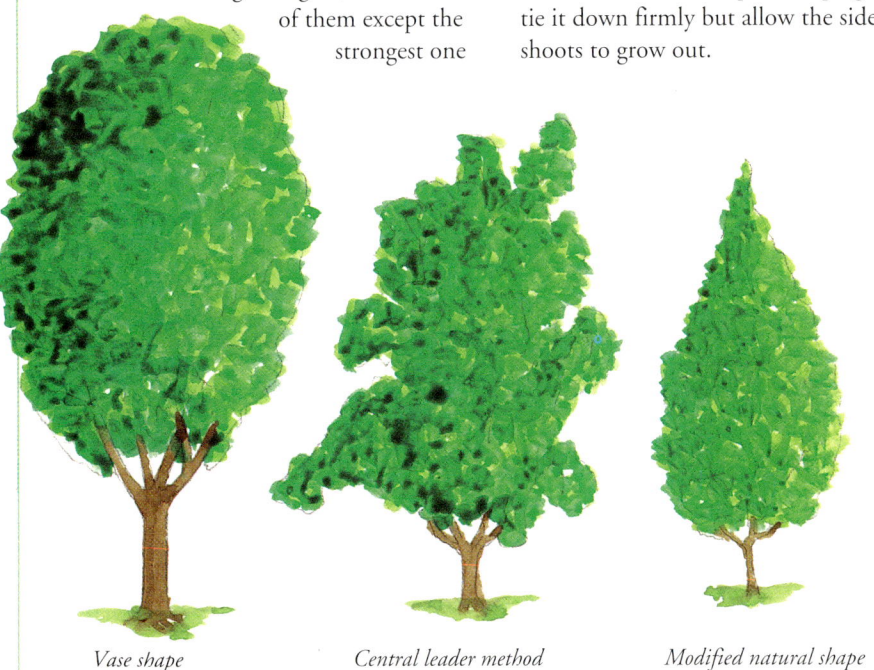

Vase shape   *Central leader method*   *Modified natural shape*

Pruning Methods

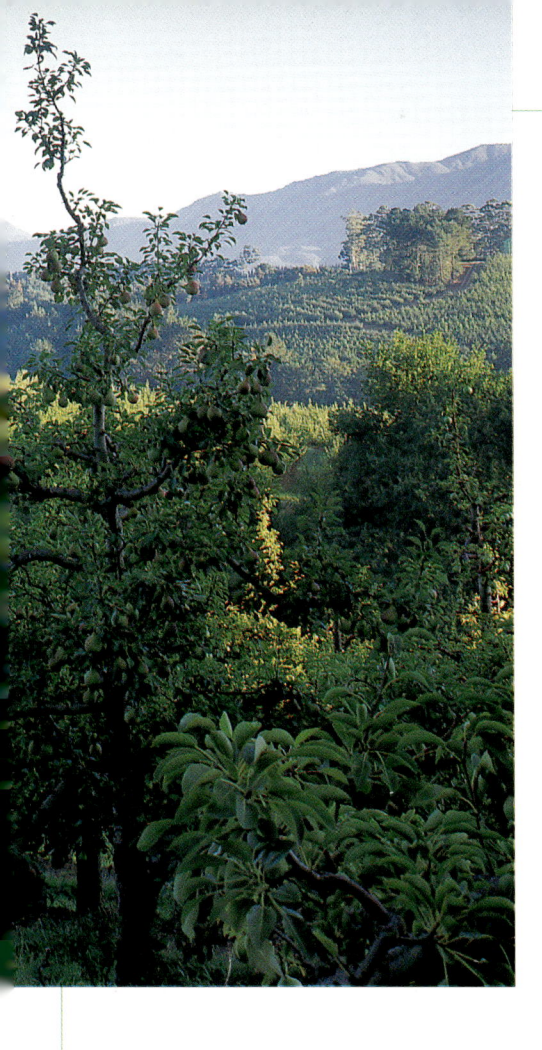

Thinning fruit

When grown well, many fruit trees produce an abundance of fruit. However, if all the fruit which sets is allowed to develop, most of it will be small and sometimes of an inferior quality. To secure crops of good sized fruit, loaded branches should therefore be thinned out. Although this may seem rather drastic, the results are worth it.

Thinning of fruit is best done in two stages, especially for the very heavy bearers such as plums and peaches. Start by thinning out the young fruits when they are about the size of a marble and then again when they are egg-sized. Leave about 8-10 cm between small-fruited plums and apricots and 15 cm between larger plums and apricots, peaches, pears and apples. Bunches of grapes should be thinned to about 45 cm. Heavy bearing citrus should be thinned so that the fruit is more evenly distributed and only one or two fruits hang from a shoot.

Pinching out

Although not often thought of as part of the pruning process, pinching out is an important part of your pruning programme. This method is especially used on softwooded plants, such as granadillas, to make them bush out. Trees and shrubs which do not require any hard pruning can nevertheless be pinched back in order to keep them in good shape.

Pruning hints

◆ Before making any pruning cuts, check your tools for sharpness. Cuts made with blunt secateurs or pruners may leave jagged edges which could become infected with fungal diseases.
◆ Prune back a shoot just above an outward-facing growth bud. Make the cut about 1-2 cm above the bud. Long stubs can cause dieback of the stem.
◆ When pruning dead or diseased wood, cut below the diseased or dead portion into healthy growth. After pruning a diseased plant, remember to clean pruning tools in disinfectant.
◆ Take great care when cutting off any large branches. When a branch is too heavy to be supported with your hand, trying to cut it off next to the main branch or trunk can lead to the splitting and stripping of the bark. To prevent this, first cut off the unwanted branch about 30 cm from the trunk, then carefully saw off the stub close to the stem by cutting upwards through the stub as far as you can, then downwards to meet the first cut. This will give you a clean surface without any torn bark.
◆ Painting the cut with a sealing compound if it is larger than 5-8 cm in diameter will help prevent fungal diseases and cankers.

Make a neat, sharp cut just above the bud.

This is a bad cut – too slanted and close to the bud.

This is also a bad cut – it is too slanted a slit with rough edges which could cause the branch to die back.

The first thinning is done when the fruit is very small, about marble-sized.

The second thinning is done once the fruit has developed to about egg-size.

Well-spaced fruit.

Dwarf fruit trees, different vegetables and herbs are ideal crop-producing container plants.

PLANT THEM IN POTS

It is not essential to have a garden in order to grow edible crops. As long as you have an area which gets about four to five hours of sun a day, whether it be on a patio, balcony or paved courtyard, you will be able to grow a wide range of vegetables, as well as smaller growing fruit trees and creepers. Even if you do have a garden, you might not have the right growing conditions (especially for vegetables), such as insufficient sun, poor soil or too much wind – growing the plants in containers will overcome these problems.

Growing plants in containers has a number of advantages. While you may not be able to produce a large quantity of fruit or vegetables at a time, the plants are often easier to care for and protect from insect attack than those in the open ground.

Filling the containers with the correct soil is less hard work than having to dig properly prepared beds and planting holes, especially for vegetables. It is also easier to ensure that each particular type has its own specific growing medium, for example, tomatoes need a very rich, well-composted and manured soil, but carrots like a light, very friable soil.

CONTAINER CHOICE

Almost any object that can hold soil but allows water to drain out can be used as a container. This ranges from plastic and metal tins, black plastic plant bags, old metal or rubber garbage bins, metal barrels, old baths, a stack of car tyres, to specially made plastic, asbestos, cement and terracotta pots, containers, troughs and window boxes, as well as grow bags.

The size of the container you use will depend on the type of vegetable you wish to grow. Shallow root crops, such as lettuce, spring onions and many herbs, can be grown in pots or containers which are between 20-50 cm deep; long troughs, flower boxes and wide, square containers are an excellent choice. Plants with a deep root system as well as climbing types should be grown in large, deep containers.

HOW TO PLANT A STRAWBERRY BARREL

1. Make sure the strawberry barrel has adequate drainage holes.
2. Put in a 5 cm layer of small stones or stone chips for drainage.
3. Fill the barrel with good compost-enriched potting soil to just below the first set of holes.
4. Push the strawberry plants through the holes from the inside of the pot with the roots just below the holes. Fill with more soil, making sure that the roots are firmly anchored, and water well. Fill with soil again to the next set of holes.
5. Continue in this way, filling up to the top of the barrel, then plant three strawberries at the top. Water well.

WHAT IS A GROW BAG?

Many overseas gardeners grow vegetables, especially tomatoes, peppers, eggplants, climbing cucumbers and courgettes, in grow bags. These are commercially made plastic bags filled with a rich growing medium. On one of the flat sides of the plastic bag are small holes for drainage, while on the other there are holes for planting.

Not yet readily available locally, grow bags are easy to make. Take a large plastic bag such as an old 30 dm compost bag or a 20 kg fertilizer bag. Fill it three-quarters full with a rich, well-composted potting soil. Seal the ends well with tape. Make small drainage holes on one side, about 20 cm apart. Put your grow bag, with the drainage holes facing down, on any kind of flat surface which gets about three to five hours of sun. Morning sun is better than afternoon sun, especially in summer. Make holes in the top surface of the bag and plant your young established seedlings into them. Two holes per bag is the recommended number for plants such as tomatoes, peppers or eggplants.

Strawberry plants are planted in each of the holes with three plants on the top.

A grow bag is an easy way to grow vegetables in a small space.

Soil and drainage

To grow well in containers, plants must get enough of the essential plant nutrients. While the soil must hold water and not dry out too rapidly, it must not become waterlogged either. Plants grown in containers will not do well if there is poor drainage, so the soil itself must drain well and the containers must have proper drainage holes. Make sure that the containers have adequate drainage holes before you plant – trying to improve drainage once a container has been planted is extremely difficult.

The individual holes should be about 1-2 cm wide and the number of holes will depend on the size of the container. A trough 90 cm long usually has eight drainage holes, while round or square pots may have one large hole in the centre or three to five holes spaced around the bottom. The drainage holes must be covered to stop the soil blocking the holes. Use broken brick, small stones, pebbles or stone chips, but do not use bits of concrete – concrete has too much lime in it and the chemical leaches out onto the plants. It is a good idea to raise large containers a few centimetres off the ground by putting small pieces of flat stone under the containers to prevent weeds or debris from blocking the drainage holes.

Either buy ready-made potting soil for your containers or make your own. If you feel that a ready-made soil is not rich enough for a specific vegetable, add extra compost or old manure, while coarse sand can be added to make the mixture finer and more friable.

What to grow in your containers

If you want to grow edible crops in containers, usually the best and most rewarding results are from vegetables. Certain fruit trees can also be grown in containers but do not produce as well as they would in the open ground.

Citrus, however, especially the dwarf varieties of lemons, oranges and naartjies, as well as kumquats and calamondins, grow well in containers and make extremely attractive container subjects. Quick-growing climbers like granadillas can also be grown.

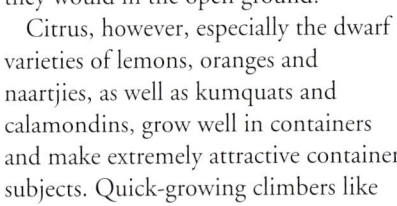

To ensure good drainage, put down layers of stones, then fill the container with the correct soil.

Which vegetables to choose

The quick-growing, quick-maturing crops and the 'cut-and-come-again' vegetables are the best choice. Most salad crops are extremely successful and popular because of their good flavour when freshly picked. Only one or two tomato plants and peppers can provide you with plenty of fruit over a relatively long period, while a long trough of loose-leaf lettuce will go on producing leaves for months on end. Many of the spreading vegetables, such as cucumbers and courgettes, are easily trained up a trellis or wall, while climbing beans and peas take up less room than bush types.

Always be as selective as possible when choosing the actual cultivars. Many of the newer hybrids have been specially bred for container growing and it is worthwhile trying to get hold of them rather than the older types.

Potting soil recipe

2 parts garden soil
1 part coarse sand
1 part sieved compost or peat

Add 30 g of balanced fertilizer, such as 2.3.2, to each bucketful of the mixture, or use a generous handful of old manure and about 30 g of bone meal.

Container candidates

Beans – climbing
Beetroot
Broccoli
Cabbage – small head
Carrots – short rooted
Cucumber
Eggplant
Lettuce

Containers of various shapes and sizes can be used for vegetables and small fruit trees.

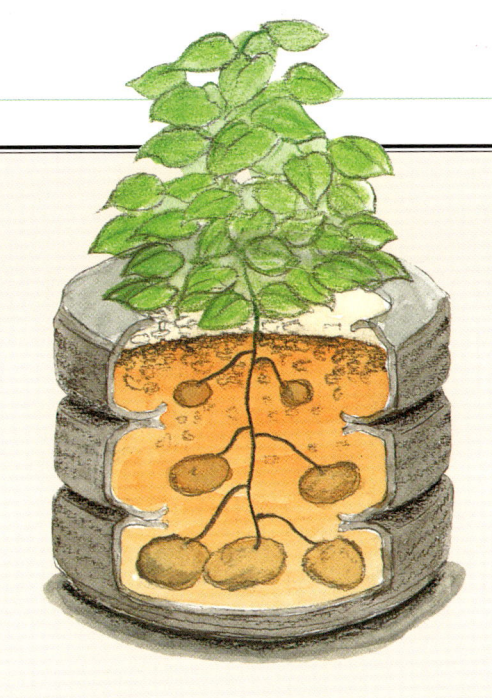

POTATOES IN CONTAINERS

If you do not have enough space in your garden or the right position for potatoes, you can solve the problem by growing your potatoes in a number of novel ways (such as in barrels or plastic bags), one of the easiest being to grow them in tyres.

To grow potatoes in tyres, follow these simple steps:
1. Place a car tyre on the ground or on a paved surface in a sunny position. Fill it up almost to the top with well-composted soil and add a tablespoon of 2.3.2 fertilizer.
2. Put about four or five sprouted seed potatoes into the soil and then cover with about 5 cm of soil; water well.
3. Keep the soil damp and when the shoots appear and have grown about 10 cm above the top of the tyre, put on another tyre and gently fill it in with well-composted soil, taking care not to break the plants. Feed the plants with a liquid fertilizer. Keep the soil damp.
4. When the plants grow through the soil again, put on another tyre and fill it up. Feed again with a liquid fertilizer. You may be able to put on a fourth tyre before the plants start to flower. Keep the soil damp.
5. Once the plants have flowered and the foliage begins to turn yellow, you should harvest your crop.

From one set of tyres you can get up to 5-6 kg of baby or new potatoes – large storage potatoes are not suited to this growing method. You can also grow baby potatoes in thick black plastic bags or large drums, following the basic steps of covering up the potatoes as they grow.

Peas – climbing
Peppers
Potatoes
Radish
Spinach
Swiss chard spinach
Tomatoes, especially determinate and small-fruited types
Turnips

See pages 41-77 for more detailed information on the individual types.

CONTAINER CARE

It is important to realize that plants in containers usually dry out far more quickly than plants in the ground. This is mainly because the surface and the sides of the container are exposed to the sun. As containers are often placed on a paved surface, this also reflects the heat, as do surrounding walls, particularly white painted ones.

Water your container plants regularly. It is far better to check your soil than to follow a hard and fast rule of watering every day, twice a week or every five days. The quality of vegetables in particular can be spoilt if the plants dry out. Lettuces will quickly turn bitter if they get in the least bit dry. Weather conditions are an important factor in how often the plants need to be watered. Remember that when it rains, containerized plants get less water than those in the ground because of the smaller surface area – often the foliage is so dense that no rain will actually soak in.

Like all plants, your containerized ones will need regular feeding. This is especially important with vegetables as steady, vigorous growth is essential for top quality produce. While the usual granular fertilizers can be used, these are often difficult to apply to containers – too much can be applied or the foliage can be burnt. Water soluble, concentrated fertilizers, either artificial or organic, are a much easier and safer method. There are a number formulated for container plants and vegetables so follow the manufacturers' recommended rates of application and frequency. If you making liquid manure, water the plants every three to four weeks.

REPLANTING CONTAINERS

Before planting a second crop, you will have to replenish the soil as the original plants will have used up a great deal of its goodness. Small containers and troughs can easily be emptied and refilled with a fresh soil mix. This is not always practical for the larger containers. You will have to re-use most of the existing soil and add fresh material. Always take out the entire old crop, especially the roots. Loosen the soil as deeply as possible and take out at least a quarter of it. Refill the pot with a good potting mix or a rich compost. Add some old manure (fresh manure has too much nitrogen in it which could burn the plants) for the leaf crops but not for the root vegetables.

Because of the build-up of soil diseases and nematodes, try to alternate the crops in a simple form of crop rotation – this is especially important with tomatoes and potatoes. Growing marigolds in your containers for one season is another method which can help in clearing out nematodes.

Only a small space is required in the garden to grow a wide selection of vegetables.

VEGETABLES

Choosing the right position in which to grow your vegetables is vital (*see* page 9). Once you have decided on the best growing area within your garden, then the actual vegetable beds can be planned in detail. Always remember that you should have a convenient source of water near at hand in the form of a tap and hose or an irrigation system. Where water restrictions or a lack of water occur during certain times of the year, installing a rain-water tank is a good idea.

How many vegetable beds?

You do not need a large area of ground to grow vegetables. In fact, if you have never grown vegetables before, you should perhaps begin with a small plot. Start with one to two vegetable beds, depending on the needs of your family and the amount of time you have to tend to the plants. You should be able to spend a minimum of half an hour per day on watering, weeding, and so on.

Size and shape

While a vegetable bed can be any shape and size, a rectangular bed, roughly 1-1,5 m wide and 2-3 m long, is extremely practical – it is easy to work from either side without having to step into the growing plants. A smaller, door-sized bed, 1 m x 2 m, is ideal for smaller areas. Naturally, if you have enough space, you can gradually make the beds longer but not any wider. The width of the paths between the beds

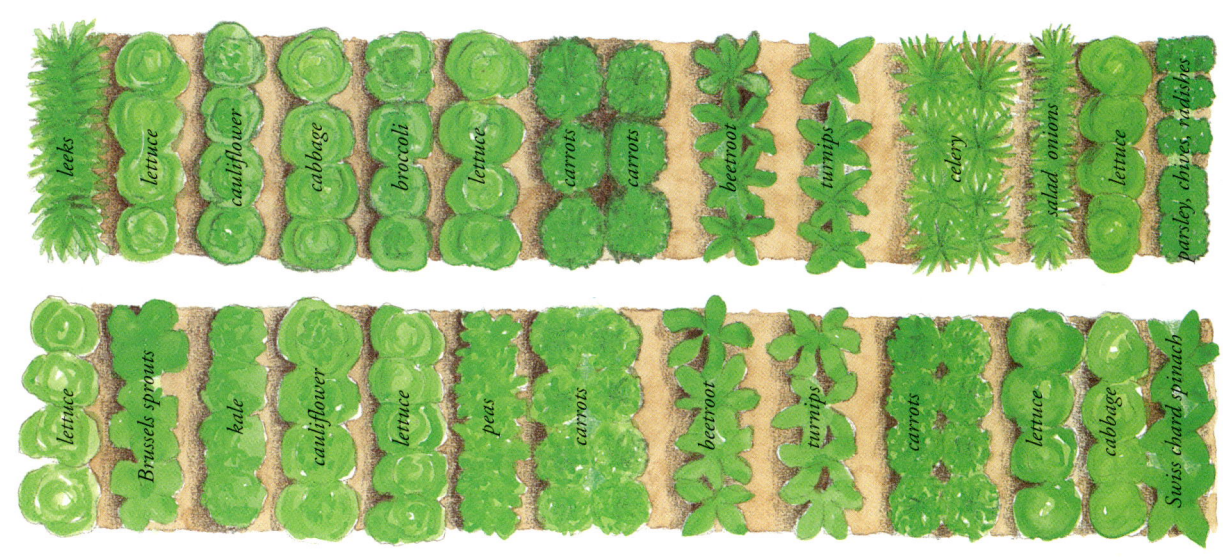

Two long beds can be planted over the whole season with a succession of sowings and plantings.

A small, door-sized bed can be used to grow a number of different vegetables.

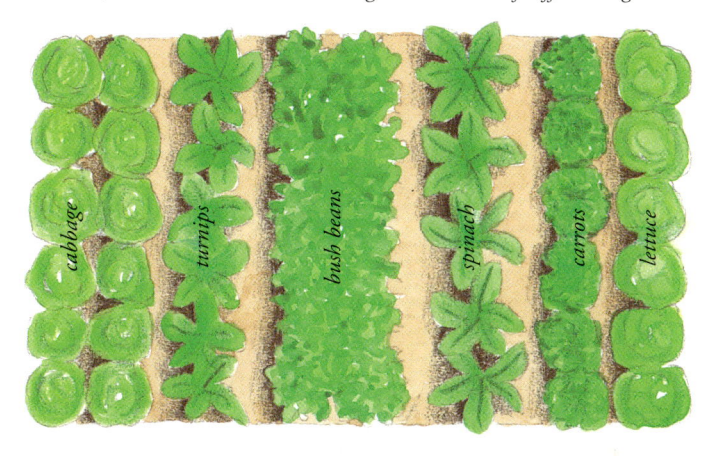

Summer and winter

For gardeners who want to concentrate on summer salad vegetables, a small 1,5 m² bed is easy to manage. Here you can grow very small quantities of lettuce, radish, tomatoes and peppers, for example. In winter the same space can be utilized for soup crops such as turnips, swedes, leeks, celery and broccoli.

Food from your Garden

A neatly laid out back garden with rectangular beds and narrow gravel pathways.

A compact vegetable bed – the T-plan gives the gardener easy access.

A vegetable bed can be any shape, depending on the space available.

Vegetables

Rows of vegetables can be separated by narrow paths between the mounded soil.

Low walls made from bricks or other similar material will contain the soil.

should be 30-50 cm. If you plan to have a number of beds, make a central path, wide enough for a wheelbarrow.

If, however, the available space does not lend itself to a series of long or even door-shaped beds, plan them, utilizing the space to its best advantage. This may mean having corner beds, square-shaped beds or even long, narrow beds. Any shape and size can prove successful, providing that the growing conditions are correct and the soil has been properly prepared.

Remember that vegetables do not have to be grown in specific beds. Many can be sown in beds and borders amongst other plants if these are the most suitable growing areas. Tomatoes, eggplants and peppers are attractive, bushy plants, while various types of loose-leaf lettuce make interesting and unusual edging plants. Climbing beans and peas can be grown up fences or trellises at the back of borders.

Preparing the ground

Never be in a hurry to plant your first crop of vegetables. Time spent in preparing the soil will result in quicker-growing, healthier plants. Although initial deep digging or trenching of the individual beds is time-consuming and fairly hard work, this does not have to be done every season – you should not have to completely re-dig a really well-prepared trench for about five years. There are various ways of preparing soil. The most important is to incorporate plenty of organic material which will decompose in the soil, as well as using ready-made compost and organic and artificial fertilizers (*see* pages 16-18).

What to grow

The main reason for growing your own vegetables is to supply your family with fresh, nutritious food. While there is a vast range of vegetables which can be grown at various times of the year, concentrate on the types which your family enjoy, which produce the biggest crops in the shortest amount of time, which take up the least amount of space, and which do not need constant

A wide variety of vegetables, such as these tomatoes, are now available in trays from nurseries.

attention or very specialized growing conditions. Beans and Swiss chard spinach, for example, are amongst the most rewarding and economical vegetables to grow. Carrots, which are fairly slow-growing, deserve a place in the garden as they have so many culinary uses. Onions, however, can take up to six months before they are ready to harvest, depending on the cultivar. Onions are also not the most rewarding of vegetables for the small home garden as highly fertile soils and favourable weather conditions are essential for good crops.

Similarly, potatoes take time and space if you want to produce mature storage potatoes, but immature 'baby' potatoes are relatively easy to grow.

High yields, small space

Beans
Broccoli
Cabbage
Carrots
Celery
Chinese cabbage
Courgettes (baby marrows)
Cucumbers – trellised
Kale
Lettuce, especially loose-leaved
Parsnips
Peas – climbing
Radish
Squash – bush
Swiss chard spinach
Turnips

Vegetables for your freezer

Beans
Beetroot
Broccoli
Brussels sprouts
Carrots
Cauliflower
Courgettes
Parsnips
Peas
Pumpkin
Spinach
Swedes
Sweetcorn
Swiss chard spinach
Tomatoes

SPRING PLANTING

SUMMER PLANTING

Summer Garden

For a succession of salad vegetables produced in a small space, start planting in spring (left). As the vegetables are harvested and the crops picked, replant as per the illustration on the right (Summer Planting).

AUTUMN PLANTING

WINTER PLANTING

Winter Garden

Once the summer crops are over, start planting as per the illustration on the left (Autumn Planting). As these are harvested, plant as per the illustration on the right (Winter Planting).

VEGETABLES

An assortment of lettuces makes a colourful display, as well as providing crops over a long period.

Neat rows of vegetables make cultivation easier.

WHEN TO PLANT

While it would be wonderful to grow your favourite vegetables throughout the year, this is not always possible as many have specific growing seasons. As temperature is an important factor, optimum planting times can vary considerably from region to region. For example, in summer rainfall regions it becomes warmer in spring quicker than it does in the winter rainfall regions. There can thus be three to four weeks difference between the start of the summer sowing season. A number of vegetables which are produced in most parts of the country during summer are grown in autumn, winter and spring in the subtropical regions, because of the heat and humidity.

CLIMATE GUIDE

Warm season vegetables – 20 °C and higher
Beans – bush
Beans – climbing
Chilli peppers
Courgettes
Cucumbers
Eggplant
Marrows
Mealies
Melons
Peppers
Potatoes
Pumpkins
Squash
Sweetcorn
Sweet potatoes
Tomatoes

Cool season vegetables – low temperatures 10-20 °C
Broad beans
Broccoli
Brussels sprouts
Cauliflowers
Chinese cabbage
Kale
Kohlrabi
Onions
Peas
Spinach

Intermediate vegetables — moderate temperatures 15-20 °C (almost year round)
Beetroot
Cabbage
Carrots
Celery
Leeks
Lettuce
Parsnips
Potatoes
Radish
Swiss chard spinach

45

Feast or famine

One of the biggest problems which home gardeners experience is that they either have too much of one type of vegetable at a time or nothing at all. The way to avoid this problem is to follow a careful programme of successive sowing (*see* individual entries) and by planting small amounts of different vegetables. This will ensure a continuous supply, plus regular empty spaces available for the next planting. Naturally, the number of successive sowings or plantings of one kind of vegetable you can make during a season will depend on the available space. The more space you have, the more can be grown.

While the number of plants recommended per planting may seem extremely small (*see* individual entries), these amounts will provide enough for the average family of that particular vegetable while it is at its best. You can, of course, plant out more if you are able to use them.

Planning tips

◆ Plant each type of vegetable in a number of short rows across the bed rather than in long, single rows which run from top to bottom.
◆ To stop the taller growing vegetables, such as mielies, climbing beans and peas, tomatoes and broad beans, casting shade over lower growing ones, plant them on the south side of the bed.
◆ Try to group vegetables which mature at the same time in one part of the bed – this makes preparing the soil for the next crop easier.
◆ Due to their different soil needs, plan a separate bed for your root crops, such as carrots and beetroot, where possible.

Planting distances

Provided your soil is well prepared, vegetables in the home garden can be planted closer together than the recommendations which are usually given for commercially grown open field crops. Nevertheless, you should be careful not to overcrowd your vegetables and each one should be given sufficient space in which to grow and mature.

Vegetables at different stages of growth give a succession of crops.

Cultivars

Once you have decided to grow your own vegetables, it is important to realize that most of the popular vegetables have a number of cultivars. The readily available types in seed packet form or sold as seedlings have been selected as suitable for home gardening. However, choose your varieties as carefully as possible to make sure they suit your particular needs and your area's growing conditions. Some vegetables, such as onions cauliflower, have early, mid-season and late cultivars which must be sown at the correct times.

It is always preferable to grow the modern cultivars and F1 hybrid seed (plants of a first generation hybrid of

SEED OR SEEDLINGS

Whether all your vegetables should be grown from seed will depend on the type of vegetable and the amount of time you have to spend on caring for seed boxes.

A number of vegetables, such as beans, peas and carrots, are best sown directly into beds where they are left to mature and are virtually never available in seedling form. However, other types such as tomatoes, cabbage, cauliflower and lettuce, are started in seed boxes or seed beds and, depending on the season, are readily available in seedling form from most nurseries and garden shops.

When only a few plants are needed at a time, sowing them from seed can be time-consuming and wasteful. It is also important to remember that commercial vegetable growers often produce seedlings of new and improved cultivars, the seed of which is not easily available in small quantities. They also concentrate on cultivars which are most suitable to their particular growing region and to the weather conditions.

CROP ROTATION AND THE SMALL GARDEN

In the modern home vegetable garden, where small quantities of a range of different vegetables are cultivated in fairly quick succession, it is difficult to follow the traditional methods of crop rotation. The following points should be followed to help ensure the fertility of your soil and stop the build-up of harmful pathogens.

◆ Avoid growing the same vegetables or closely related types in the same place for two consecutive years.
◆ Avoid continually growing plants with large root systems in the same place.
◆ Root vegetables which do better in light instead of over-rich soil should be planted after heavy feeders like peppers, tomatoes and eggplants.
◆ After a crop of leaf vegetables such as cabbage, cauliflower, broccoli and Brussels sprouts, plant legumes such as beans and peas to build up the nitrogen content of the soil.

two dissimilar parents – have hybrid vigour, have uniformly higher yields and are disease resistant) wherever possible as these usually give better quality crops and are often more disease resistant.

Many of the well-known older cultivars are still available but have been superseded by new and improved ones. While the latest cultivars regularly become available to the commercial farmer, they are not always marketed in picture packets. However, it is sometimes possible to get these special types in small quantities directly from the seed merchants. It is often well worth the extra effort to get these cultivars as in many instances you will be rewarded with vastly improved crops, as well as unusual types.

If in any doubt about which types of vegetables to grow in your area, contact your nearest seed merchant or one of the food growing organizations for expert local advice.

BEANS

Beans are among the easiest and most rewarding vegetables to grow. They are also very versatile in the kitchen – serve them hot by simply boiling them in water, or cold in one of many different bean salads. If you have more beans then your family can eat, freeze them, bottle them or make them into chutney.

Types of beans

There are two types of green beans that give particularly good results in the home garden. The first is the dwarf bean, also known as a bush bean, French bean or snap bean. They are called dwarf beans because they produce their edible pods on low, bushy plants, about 30-50 cm high. There are a number of well-known varieties of dwarf beans on the market, as well as some excellent new cultivars.

The second type is the tall-growing runner bean which can grow up to 2 m and more. Known sometimes as a climbing bean, it needs to be grown up a trellis or fence.

Quick-growing dwarf beans tend to bear up to a fortnight earlier than runner beans, but runner beans go on producing pods for longer. Many people prefer the flavour of runner beans.

Where space is limited, runner beans are the ideal choice but as beans have fairly shallow roots, better results are obtained from bush beans in areas which are very windy.

Growing beans

A warm season crop, beans are grown in most parts of South Africa during the summer months; however, they do best in the subtropical regions when sown during autumn and winter.

Beans produce the best crops when grown in well-prepared, fertile, well-drained soil. Dig the planting area over and add generous amounts of compost. To ensure the necessary quick, steady growth, add 2.3.2 fertilizer at the rate of 60 g per m² or per metre row, or use an enriched organic fertilizer.

For a good supply of dwarf beans for the average family, you will need 2 x 1,5 m rows per sowing. Depending on the size and shape of your beds, sow the equivalent of a couple of long rows or a block of short rows. The rows should be about 50-60 cm apart and the seeds should be planted 7-10 cm apart and 4-5 cm deep.

For a good crop of climbing beans, you only need a 1-3 m row per sowing with the seeds about 10-15 cm apart.

Runner beans can be grown up a wire fence or a wooden trellis. They can also be grown up a support made of two rows of stakes, strengthened by a cross pole, or up a wigwam of poles tied together at the top. Because the plants grow quickly, it is better to have the climbing support in place before you sow the seed.

Regular watering is essential for good crops of both dwarf and climbing beans. Keep the soil damp but not saturated until the seed germinates. Thereafter, keep the plants watered regularly and never let them dry out; plenty of water

Quick-growing beans are one of the most prolific of vegetables.

Beans need a support around which to twine.

Vegetables

> ## Beans at a glance
>
> **Type of plant:** Seed-bearing annual; warm season.
> **Edible parts:** Seed pods.
> **Best soil:** Fertile, well drained, pH 6,0-6,8.
> **When to plant:** Spring (after danger of frost has passed) to late summer.
> **The right amount:** Bush beans 2 x 1,5 m row per sowing. Runner beans 1 x 1,5 m row per sowing.
> **How to plant:** Dwarf beans in rows 50-60 cm apart; seed 7-10 cm apart, 4-5 cm deep. Runner beans up supports; seed 10-15 cm apart, 4-5 cm deep.
> **Care:** Regular watering, especially when plants begin to flower and set pods. Beans have shallow roots, so do not cultivate deeply near them. Water early in the morning to ensure foliage dry by nightfall or surface irrigate to help prevent fungal diseases. Do not work between bean plants when foliage is wet – can spread fungal diseases.
> **When to harvest:** 7-10 weeks after sowing, depending on type and variety.
> **How to harvest:** Carefully pull young pods from the plants.
> **Successive plantings:** Every 3-4 weeks for dwarf beans; every 6-8 weeks for runner beans.
> **Storage methods:** Freezing and bottling.

during the flowering and pod setting time is vital. Very dry conditions and low humidity can cause petal drop. A thick layer of mulch will protect the shallow roots from the heat. As dwarf beans can become heavy when carrying a large crop, drawing up extra soil around the plants will support them.

Beans should not need too much extra care if the soil was well prepared before planting. However, they do respond well to light applications of a nitrogenous fertilizer such as LAN which should be applied at the rate of 10 g per running metre. Give them two applications of LAN, one about a week to 10 days after sowing, and the second one just as they are coming into flower. Feeding will improve the pods and encourage the plants to bear over a longer period. If you prefer using organic rather than chemical products, feed the plants with home-made liquid fertilizer or a commercial liquid feed.

To encourage flowering and pod set, pinch back the growing tips of runner beans once they have reached the top of their supports.

The first of your dwarf beans should be ready to pick about 7-10 weeks after sowing, depending on the variety, and will go on producing pods for about 3 weeks. Runner beans will be ready in about 9-10 weeks after sowing and will go on producing for about 6-7 weeks as long as the pods are picked regularly and the plants are kept well fed.

Pick your beans frequently to ensure a supply of pods over as long a period as possible. If you do not get enough young pods initially for a family meal, keep the beans in the fridge until the next picking. While in full production, check the plants twice or even three times a week and pick as necessary.

As the plants are easily damaged, pick the pods carefully. Always make sure that no pods remain on the plant – pods which are allowed to grow large and make big seeds weaken the plants and stop more flowers from developing.

Possible problems

Young plants wilt and die
Cause: Cutworms
Use cutworm bait or put paper or plastic collars around plants.

Young shoots and leaves distorted – small insects on stems and leaves
Cause: Aphids
Hose off with a jet of water and spray with soap solution or herb spray. Use a vegetable-safe insecticide.

Shoots and tips wilt and die – green bugs on plants
Cause: Green shield bug
Spray with herbal spray or use a vegetable-safe insecticide and take careful note of withholding times.

Leaves go black or brown and plants wither and die
Cause: Fungal disease, e.g. anthracnose
Difficult to control once plants infected; spray with suitable fungicide.

Recommended cultivars

Dwarf beans
Contender – medium-green, good heat tolerance
Seminole – light-green, disease resistant
Strike – medium-green, very prolific
Top Crop – medium-green, similar to Seminole
Wintergreen – medium-green, winter production in warm, frost-free areas

Runner beans
Blue Peter – novelty; blue pods, turn green when cooked
Lazy Housewife – medium-green, good flavour and bearer
Witsa – medium-green, disease resistant

Utilise extra space by growing climbing beans.

Both the swollen roots and the leaves of beetroot are edible.

BEETROOT AT A GLANCE

Type of vegetable: Root; intermediate.
Edible part: Swollen roots and young leaves.
Best soil: Fertile, friable, well-drained soil, pH 6,0-7,0.
When to plant: Spring to autumn.
The right amount: 2 x 1,5 m rows.
How to plant: In rows, seeds 2,5-5 cm apart, rows 20-30 cm apart.
Care: Keep soil moist and free from weeds; thin out.
When to harvest: 8-10 weeks after sowing.
How to harvest: Dig out, pull off tops – do not cut with knife.
Successive plantings: Every 3-4 weeks.
Storage methods: Refrigerate or pickle.

BEETROOT

Popular as a pickled salad vegetable, but also served cooked hot or cold, beetroot is relatively easy to grow. While the round or globe-shaped types are the best known, there are also long, cylindrical varieties available. It is not just the roots which are edible – young beet tops can be added to salads while the larger leaves can be cooked as you would spinach.

GROWING BEETROOT

Beetroot are very adaptable and can be grown almost throughout the year but September to March are particularly good sowing months. Like all root vegetables, beetroot grow best in soil which has been well cultivated and has good drainage. They prefer a slightly acid to neutral soil. New beds should be enriched with well-decomposed compost and a dressing of 2.3.2 fertilizer. The plants also do well as a follow-on crop, especially after a crop of heavy feeders such as tomatoes.

As the seedlings do not transplant at all well, the seeds should be sown directly into the vegetable bed. To help speed up the germination period, soak the seeds overnight. Each 'seed' is actually a cluster of three to five true seeds and should be sown 2,5-5 cm apart in shallow furrows and covered by about 2,5 cm of soil. There should be about 20-30 cm between the furrows.

Mulching the soil with fine compost or old grass will help it from drying out during the initial growing stage. Sow approximately 2 x 1 m long rows every 4-5 weeks during the growing season.

As the seedlings develop, thin them out to about 3-5 cm apart. Thin out again as the roots form to 7-10 cm apart. Always keep the soil moist as a sudden lack of water can interrupt growth and spoil the quality of the crop. Beet should be ready for harvesting approximately 8-10 weeks after sowing.

First take out every other plant as this will allow the remaining ones more room to grow and so extend the harvest period. Do not allow the roots to grow to more than 5-7 cm long or they will lose flavour. When harvesting, twist off the leaves 5 cm from the top of the root.

POSSIBLE PROBLEMS

Young plants wilt and die
Cause: Cutworms
Use cutworm bait.

Black-brown spots form on leaf
Cause: Leaf spot fungal disease
Spray with suitable fungicide.

RECOMMENDED CULTIVARS

Detroit Dark Red – round, crimson-red, good flavour
Crimson Globe – round, dark-red
Formanova – cylindrical, light-red

Vegetables

Ready for picking: broccoli heads must be firm and compact before harvesting.

BROCCOLI

Of all the members of the cole or cabbage family, broccoli is the most adaptable and one of the easiest to grow. Broccoli is also one of the 'cut-and-come-again' vegetables as it produces numerous side shoots once the main head has been picked. Found in varying shades of grey-green, all varieties turn dark green when cooked.

Growing broccoli

Broccoli is a cool season vegetable which needs cool, moist conditions in order to develop good compact heads. The main sowing time is from mid- to late summer and the seedlings are ready for transplanting 4-6 weeks after sowing. As you need only 3-6 plants per planting, it may be quicker and easier to buy seedlings. Only plant small, sturdy seedlings. Seedlings which have been in small punnets for too long may be stunted. Like all the members of the cole and cabbage family, broccoli needs a well-prepared, deeply dug soil. As well as generous dressings of compost and old manure, add 60-70 g of 2.3.2 fertilizer. As the plants prefer a pH level of 6,5-7,0, acid soils may need lime to raise the pH levels.

Plant the seedlings 45-50 cm apart with 45-60 cm between the rows. Make sure the soil stays moist for steady growth. About 4 weeks after planting, feed with a high nitrogen fertilizer such as LAN at the rate of 60 g per m^2. Feed again after the first heads are cut.

Harvest the main heads with about 15 cm of stem when the flower buds are fully swollen but the head is still compact – usually 9-10 weeks after transplanting. Foliar feed once the main stem is harvested. Many side shoots will develop and their heads should be cut once they reach the right stage.

Broccoli at a glance

Type of vegetable: Bud-forming; cool season.
Edible part: Flower buds; stems.
Best soil: Fertile, very well-prepared, pH 6,5-7.
When to plant: Sow mid- to late summer and autumn; plant late summer to autumn and winter.
The right amount: 3-6 plants per planting.
How to plant: Individual transplants; 45-50 cm apart.
Care: Keep moist at all times; feed twice during growing season.
When to harvest: 9-10 weeks from transplanting.
How to harvest: Cut heads when still compact.
Successive plantings: Every 4-6 weeks, depending on climate. (*Note:* Sometimes only one planting is possible.)
Storage methods: Refrigerate or freeze.

Aphids cause the crinkling of broccoli leaves.

Possible problems

Leaves crumpled and distorted
Cause: Aphids
Hose off with a jet of water, spray with soap solution or herbal spray. Use a vegetable-safe insecticide.

Holes in leaves
Cause: Various caterpillars
Hand-pick where possible. Use a herbal spray or a vegetable-safe insecticide.

Recommended cultivar

Calabrese

Red leaved cabbage makes an attractive addition to the garden and the table.

CABBAGE

Rich in minerals and vitamins, cabbage is one of the oldest and most widely grown vegetables. There are many more ways of using a cabbage than the dull, often flavourless, boiled method. Cabbages, in order to keep their flavour and looks, should be lightly boiled, steamed, braised, stir-fried, stuffed or used in soups, salads and stews.

TYPES OF CABBAGES

Cabbages are classified according to the shape of their heads, thus there are pointed, round or flat-headed types. For the home garden, the most suitable are the pointed (spitzkop) and round-headed cabbages – the drum-heads tend to grow very large, need a great deal of space and mature slowly. As there are early and late maturing types with small and medium sized heads, the actual varieties should be chosen with care. The newer hybrids are normally more vigorous and reliable than the older, better known types. Cabbages are neither only green in colour, nor do they only have smooth leaves – you can grow red- and crinkly-leaved ones too.

GROWING CABBAGES

Although a member of the cool season family, cabbages are versatile and can be grown almost throughout the year, except in very hot summer regions.

Because they should grow rapidly for the best results and are very greedy and must not dry out, cabbages need very well-prepared, well-composted soil with a pH of about 6-7. Cabbage seed should be sown into seed boxes or seed beds. As they are such popular vegetables, seedlings are usually readily available. Set out about 3-6 seedlings at each planting and make successive plantings 3-4 weeks apart. The actual spacing depends on the type. Small-headed cabbages should be planted 25 cm apart; small to medium ones should be 35 cm apart and larger heads 45 cm apart.

The plants should be watered well while the heads are developing but heavy overhead watering should be avoided once the heads have matured. Mulching the soil with compost, straw or dried grass will help keep the soil damp. For the best results feed the plants every 3 weeks with a high nitrogen fertilizer or a liquid feed. As cabbages resent root disturbance, carefully remove weeds by hand.

Pick the heads when they feel firm, usually about 10-16 weeks after transplanting, depending on the variety. Start by picking one or two small heads, enough for a meal, rather than waiting for all the plants to be the same size or you may have a glut. After cutting the heads, pull out the stalks as these provide the ideal living space for various insect pests.

CABBAGES AT A GLANCE

Type of vegetable: Leafy; intermediate.
Edible parts: Leafy heads.
Best soil: Well drained, very fertile, pH 6-7.
When to plant: Almost all year.
The right amount: 3-6 plants per transplanting.
How to plant: Seedlings 25-45 cm apart, depending on type.
Care: Water regularly, feed every 3 weeks, keep soil disturbance to a minimum.
When to harvest: 10-16 weeks after transplanting as soon as heads are firm to the touch.
How to harvest: Cut heads.
Successive plantings: 3-4 weeks.
Storage: Refrigeration.

CABBAGE SALAD

1 small, firm cabbage
1 onion, chopped
45 ml prepared French dressing
5 ml caraway seeds
5 ml dried marjoram
15 ml chopped parsley

Trim cabbage by removing the outer leaves. Wash well and shred fairly finely. Put into a bowl and pour boiling water over to cover. Allow to stand for about 10 minutes, then drain and add chopped onion.

Add caraway seeds and marjoram to French dressing. Pour this mixture over the cabbage. Chill in refrigerator until ready to serve. Sprinkle salad with the chopped parsley just before serving.
SERVES 4

Possible problems

Holes on the leaves, right through into the hearts
Cause: Caterpillars, usually cabbage white butterfly caterpillars and greater cabbage moth caterpillars. Slugs and snails are also often the cause.

Hand-pick if possible and use non-chemical or herbal sprays. Use suitable chemical insecticide and make a careful note of the withholding periods. Put out bait for slugs and snails.

Discoloration of the leaves, stunted growth, stems go black and rot off
Cause: Fungal diseases
Difficult to control. Use disease-resistant varieties; ensure good drainage; do not plant cabbages again in infected soil for at least two seasons.

Recommended cultivars

Maturity
Early – Early Jersey Wakefield, Perfection Cross, Stonehead, Spitzkool
Medium – Big Cropper, Green Star, Grand Slam, Cape Spitzkool
Late – Hercules, Green Star, Green Coronet

Note: There are many cultivars on the market, but the newer hybrids give better results and are quicker to mature.

A sturdy stand of well grown cabbages, with mealies and tomatoes alongside.

CARROTS

Among the most nutritious of vegetables because of their high vitamin A content, carrots are the leading root vegetable. They have a wide range of uses – raw as a salad vegetable, cooked as a separate dish, made into soup or added to mixed soups, stews and casseroles.

GROWING CARROTS

Carrots can be sown almost throughout the year with the winter months of May to July being the least favourable in the colder areas. While they can be grown in many types of soils, they prefer a pH of about 6-6,5 and need a deep, well-worked, fairly loose soil so that the roots will grow quickly and not be misshapen or stunted. Light, sandy loam soils are ideal for the long, cylindrical carrots while the short, stump-rooted types should be grown in shallow, very heavy soil. Add a pre-planting dressing of 2.3.4 at the rate of 60 g per 1,5 m double row.

As good drainage is important, carrots should be grown in raised beds unless the soil is especially sandy. The seed is sown directly into the bed. The furrows should be about 1 cm deep and the rows can be 15-30 cm apart. Quicker growing, smaller-rooted types can be closer together than the bigger ones. Keep the soil damp and, as snails and slugs can decimate emerging seedlings, protect them with snail bait or other pest control methods. Thin the seedlings, once two or three true leaves appear, to about 2-3 cm apart. Thin them again once they are about 15 cm tall to about 5-7 cm. While it may seem wasteful, proper thinning will yield a better crop. The small roots from the second thinning are often big enough to eat. Carrots should be ready to pick in about 8-16 weeks, depending on the variety and the weather conditions. Do not leave them in for too long – young or baby carrots have a much better flavour and texture than older ones.

Nutritious carrots, the back-bone of a vegetable garden, have many uses.

POSSIBLE PROBLEMS

Roots develop green shoulders
Cause: Exposure to the sun
Bank soil over the roots.

Roots are split or deformed
Cause: Over-rich soil

Plants make plenty of top growth but roots small and underdeveloped
Cause: Over-rich soil and not enough potassium
Use a liquid fertilizer high in potassium but low in nitrogen.

RECOMMENDED CULTIVARS

Buror
Cape Market
Chantenay Karoo
Ideal Red
Kuroda
Oxheart
Paris 108
Scarlet Nantes

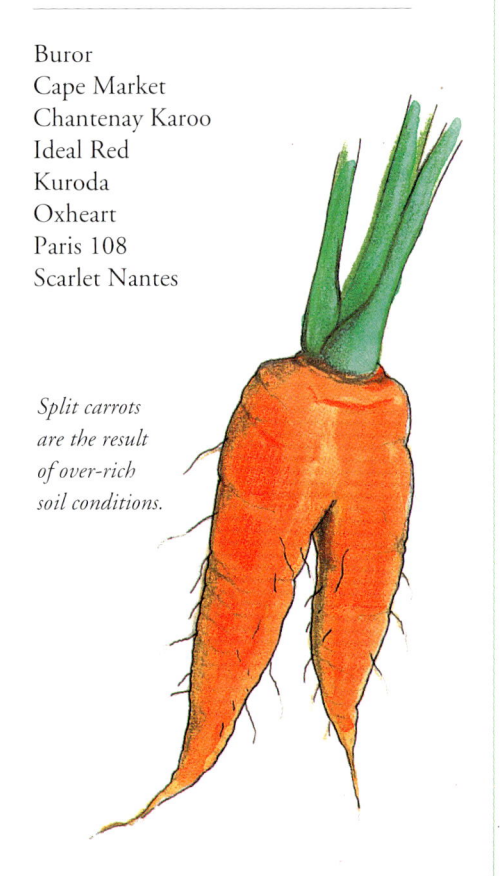

Split carrots are the result of over-rich soil conditions.

CARROTS AT A GLANCE

Type of vegetable: Root crop; intermediate.
Edible parts: Root.
Best soil: Very friable sandy loam – no fresh manure; pH 6-6,5.
When to plant: Almost all year with May, June and July least favourable in cold inland areas.
The right amount: 2 x 1,5 m rows.
How to plant: Sow thinly in shallow furrows; rows 15-30 cm apart.
Care: Regular watering; thin out; feed with 1 tbsp of LAN 4-6 weeks after sowing.
When to harvest: 8-16 weeks after sowing.
How to harvest: Carefully pull out largest ones, leaving smaller ones to continue growing.
Successive planting: 3-4 weeks.
Storage methods: Refrigerate or freeze.
Companion plants: Sage, garlic, chives and dill.

CAULIFLOWER

High in vitamin C and iron, one serving of cauliflower will provide the recommended daily dose of Vitamin C. A versatile vegetable, cauliflower can be cooked and served on its own, covered with a delicious white cheese sauce, used in a salad or made into a pickle.

Growing cauliflower

To grow top-quality cauliflowers, you must provide them with the best possible growing conditions. They are the least reliable of all the brassicas and need a very rich, slightly alkaline soil and should suffer no checks in growth due to lack of moisture or sudden changes in temperature. Cauliflower seed should be sown from mid-summer to autumn and great care should be taken to sow or plant the correct cultivars as there are early, mid-season and late types. The soil must be extremely well-prepared with compost, manure and a pre-planting dressing of 2.3.4 at the rate of 100 g per m². As cauliflowers also do best in slightly alkaline soils (pH 6,5-7), very acid soils may need added lime to increase the alkalinity. Sturdy young transplants should be set out about 50-75 cm apart, depending on the size of the heads. About one month after transplanting, give the plants a side-dressing of LAN at the rate of 60 g per every three to four plants. Work the fertilizer in well and water thoroughly. Another option is to use an enriched organic fertilizer. The plants should then be fed again approximately 3-4 weeks later.

To help keep the cauliflower heads white, fold the leaves over each other.

Once the heads have reached about 7,5-10 cm in diameter, the outer leaves can be folded over them to protect the heads from heat and wind damage. The heads are ready to harvest when they become uneven and lumpy but are still firm. Do not leave them too long or the heads will start to branch out and the quality and flavour will be spoilt. Early cultivars should be ready for harvesting about 7-10 weeks after transplanting; mid-season types take 12-15 weeks and late types up to 20 weeks and longer.

Possible problems

Leaves curled and distorted
Cause: Aphids
Spray with a strong jet of water; spray with soap solution or herbal spray. Use a suitable insecticide and note withholding period.

Holes in leaves and head eaten
Cause: Caterpillars, especially diamond-back caterpillar and greater cabbage moth caterpillar
Hand-pick where possible; spray with herbal spray or use a suitable insecticide and note withholding period.

Heads discoloured
Cause: Sunburn and lack of water
Fold a few outer leaves over head; keep very well watered.

Leaves distorted and narrow with blisters on leaf margin
Cause: Whip-tail disease due to lack of molybdenum in acid soil
No cure but seedlings can be foliar fed with sodium molybdate.

Recommended cultivars

Maturity
Early – Extra Early Six Weeks, Rami
Mid-season – Snowball
Late season – Snowcap
Note: Newer improved hybrids are available from seed merchants and as transplants in some areas, for example, Wallaby, Spring Snow and White Contessa.

These snowy white cauliflower heads are just ready for harvesting.

CAULIFLOWERS AT A GLANCE

Type of vegetable: Head-forming leaf; cool season.
Edible parts: Solid head.
Best soil: Well worked, very well composted; pH 6,5-7.
When to plant: Mid- to late summer.
The right amount: 3-6 plants per planting.
How to plant: 50-75 cm apart, depending on cultivar.
Care: Keep regularly watered; side feed with LAN; avoid cultivation near roots. Cover heads with outer leaves.
When to harvest: 7-20 weeks, depending on cultivar, when heads are firm and still lumpy.
How to harvest: Cut whole head.
Successive planting: 3-4 weeks.
Storage methods: Refrigerate.

CAULIFLOWER CHEESE

1 medium cauliflower
30 g butter
30 g flour
425 ml milk
pinch salt and pepper
100 g Cheddar cheese, grated
4 hard-boiled eggs, peeled
100 g tomatoes, halved and fried

Make a cut across the bottom of the cauliflower stalk – this reduces cooking time. Boil in salted water for about 15-20 minutes, until just soft. Drain and place in an ovenproof dish.

Make a white sauce by melting the butter over medium heat. Stir in the flour and gradually add the milk to form a smooth sauce, stirring constantly to prevent lumps from forming. Season with salt and pepper. Add 50 g of the grated cheese to the sauce and stir in thoroughly.

Cut three of the hard-boiled eggs into quarters and arrange around the cauliflower along with the tomatoes, reserving a few of each for garnish. Pour over the white sauce, sprinkle with the remaining cheese and garnish with the rest of the eggs and tomatoes.

Grill for 5 minutes until golden-brown. Serve piping hot.
SERVES 4

Versatile courgettes develop from large, showy yellow flowers.

COURGETTES

Courgettes, also known as baby marrows or zucchini, are simply the young immature fruit of the bush marrow. They make a fine-textured cooked vegetable and can also be eaten raw in a variety of salads.

GROWING COURGETTES

Courgettes, like other summer marrows and squash, are warm season crops which should be sown from spring to mid-summer in most areas, but from late summer to late winter in the subtropical regions.

They like a rich, well-drained soil. Dig individual planting holes, 45 cm square and 30 cm deep, loosen the bottom of the hole with a fork and remove the soil. Add two spadefuls of a half and half compost/manure mixture, plus a handful of 2.3.2 fertilizer to the soil dug from the hole. Mix together

Vegetables

Courgettes need protection against attack by powdery mildew, shown here on the leaves.

> ## Courgettes at a glance
>
> **Type of vegetable:** Fleshy fruit; warm season.
> **Edible parts:** Immature fruits.
> **Best soil:** Rich, well-drained, sandy loam; pH 6-7,5.
> **When to plant:** From spring to mid-summer.
> **The right amount:** 2-3 per sowing.
> **How to plant:** Plant seeds onto well-prepared mound or 'hill'.
> **Care:** Surface water regularly; feed with high nitrogen; spray against mildew.
> **When to harvest:** 8-10 weeks when fruit is 10-15 cm long.
> **How to harvest:** Cut off with sharp knife, leaving short stalk on the fruit.
> **Successive plantings:** 4-6 weeks.
> **Storage:** Refrigerate.

and put back into the hole so that the soil mixture forms a mound or 'hill'. Sow three to four seeds on each hill. Once the seed has germinated, thin to the distance of the two seeds furthest apart. If seedlings are available, plant two per hill.

Keep plants well watered as they will dry out very rapidly due to their large leaves. Mulch with compost to help conserve water and discourage weeds. Feed with 1 teaspoon of LAN once the plants have developed three to four true leaves. Repeat every 4-6 weeks once the plants begin to flower. Courgettes are very prone to mildew so surface irrigate and regularly dust the large leaves with dusting sulphur or spray with a suitable fungicide. Remove badly infected old leaves and any fruit stung by fruit fly.

The courgettes should be ready to harvest 8-10 weeks after sowing when the fruit is about 10-15 cm long. Allow them to develop to 25-30 cm long but no bigger or they will become coarse and stringy.

Possible problems

White deposit on leaves which then go brown and dry out
Cause: Powdery mildew
Surface irrigate especially in hot, humid conditions. Pick off some of the leaves if the plants are very leafy to allow in more light and air. Dust regularly with dusting sulphur or otherwise spray with a suitable fungicide from when the plant has two to three leaves.

Leaves mottled with yellow patches and fall off
Cause: Red spider mite
Keep plants well mulched to increase humidity, especially in hot dry weather. Spray undersides of leaves with herbal spray or use a suitable systemic insecticide but note withholding period.

Poor fruit set
Cause: Lack of insect pollinators, such as bees, usually due to overcast and inclement weather; will improve again once weather warm and sunny.

Fruit has holes and falls off
Cause: Fruit fly
Use a suitable fruit fly bait.

Recommended cultivars

Ambassador
Caserta
Notes:
◆ Try to get the seed of special hybrids such as Elite, Emperor or Longzini.
◆ Other small-growing bush marrows and squashes, such as Patty Pans and Gem Squash, are grown in the same way but always harvest them when young.

Young cucumbers (left) have prickles on the skin which disappear as they mature (right).

CUCUMBERS

Although cucumbers have little actual food value, their cool refreshing taste makes them an integral part of summer salads. Thinly sliced cucumber makes an excellent filling for sandwiches, while cucumber soup is delightful.

Growing cucumbers

Cucumbers need warm conditions and the best planting times are from August to December in most regions. In cooler regions, the seed can be sown into small individual pots placed in a protected spot and transplanted when conditions are much warmer. In subtropical areas, cucumbers are grown as a winter crop.

As cucumbers need plenty of space when grown flat on the ground, they are not an easy crop to fit into the home garden. They can, however, be trained up a frame, fence or trellis which takes up little space. The supports should be about 2 m high. Cucumbers are also good container candidates.

To make the necessary quick, steady growth, cucumbers need a well-prepared and well-drained soil, so add plenty of compost, well-rotted manure and a dressing of 2.3.2 fertilizer or an enriched organic product.

The seed can either be sown directly into the ground or can be raised in individual pots and then transplanted. When sowing directly into the ground along the support, sow a clump of 3-5 seeds about 2 cm deep with 60 cm-1m between clumps. Once the seed has germinated, pull out the weaker ones leaving just one or two very strong plants. When using transplants, plant the individual plants approximately 60 cm-1 m apart.

Carefully tie the stems to the support and pinch out the growing tips when the plants have produced five or six true leaves to encourage side branches. Water the plants regularly as a lack of water could lead to poor flowering. Be careful not to over-water. Only surface watering will help reduce the incidence of mildew. Spread a layer of compost around the plants without letting it touch the stems.

When the plants begin to flower and form fruit, feed them with a high nitrogen liquid feed or give a small side-dressing of LAN – 25 g per m^2. Water LAN in well – do not let the fertilizer

Cucumbers at a glance

Type of vegetable: Fleshy fruited trailer; warm season.
Edible parts: Fruit.
Best soil: Rich, well drained; pH 5,5-6,5.
When to plant: Spring to mid-summer; winter in subtropical regions.
The right amount: 3-5 plants.
How to plant: Clumps of 3-5 seeds or individual seedlings.
Care: Regular watering; feed with high nitrogen; mulch with compost.
When to harvest: 8-10 weeks after sowing.
How to harvest: Cut fruit with sharp knife.
Successive plantings: One or two sowings, 6-8 weeks apart.
Storage: Refrigerate.

Cucumbers will easily cover a sturdy frame.

touch the foliage. Repeat after 3-4 weeks. Pinch out growing tips once the main stems reach the top of the support.

Cucumbers should be ready to harvest 8-10 weeks after sowing, depending on the cultivar and the weather conditions. Cut the fruit with a sharp knife – the plants are easily damaged – and cut as soon as they are large enough for use. Do not leave any on the plant to mature as this will prevent the formation of more flowers.

Possible problems

White powdery deposit on leaves
Cause: Powdery mildew
Surface irrigate; pick off old infected leaves. Spray with suitable fungicide.

Leaves become mottled with yellow patches, minute red dots on undersides
Cause: Red spider mite
Mulch with compost and keep soil damp to encourage humidity. Spray with herbal spray or use a suitable systemic insecticide – make careful note of withholding period.

Not many fruits form
Cause: Not enough female flowers
Try to use only modern hybrid seed which is either all female or has a high percentage of female flowers. Pinch back over-long side shoots to encourage more fruiting side growth.

Leaves eaten by large ladybird-like insects
Cause: Pumpkin ladybird
Hand-pick if possible; use a herbal spray or suitable insecticide for chewing insects and note withholding period.

Young fruit has small holes, drops off
Cause: Fruit fly
Use a suitable fruit fly bait from the time the fruit first starts to form.

Recommended cultivars

Ashley
Cherokee 7

Note: Buy special hybrids from your nursery, e.g. Pepinex or Sweet Slice

Iced cucumber soup

1 small onion
750 ml vegetable stock
1 large cucumber
1 sprig mint
salt and pepper to taste
1 level tsp arrowroot
4 tbsp fresh cream
a drop of green colouring (optional)

Chop the onion finely and simmer for 15 minutes in a saucepan with the stock. Peel the cucumber and cut into small pieces, reserving some for garnish. Add to the stock with the mint and simmer until cucumber is tender. Sieve the soup, return to the pan and season well.

Blend the arrowroot and cream together. Add to the soup and slowly reheat to boiling point. Pour into a large bowl to cool.

Tint soup with colouring if using and chill in the fridge. Serve sprinkled with diced cucumber and chopped mint.
SERVES 4-6

LEEKS

With their special, mild flavour, leeks deserve to be more widely grown in the home garden. As members of the onion family they produce slender white bulbs and have a cylindrical stem surrounded by broad, flat leaves.

Leeks are easier to grow than most of their onion relatives.

Growing leeks

Leeks are less fussy about climatic conditions than their onion cousins. Although they do best when sown from late summer to autumn, an early spring sowing can also give good results. Leeks need a rich, well-prepared and deeply dug soil with a pH of between 6,5-7. Use plenty of compost and old manure, plus a dressing of 2.3.2 fertilizer. Very acid soil should be treated with lime prior to planting to adjust the pH levels.

For the best results, sow leeks into seed boxes or seedling trays, or buy transplants. Transplant them when they are 15 cm tall and the stems are as thick as a pencil. Make holes in the bed about 15-20 cm deep, 2-3 cm wide and 15 cm apart, in either short or long rows with 35 cm between them. Remove the young seedlings very carefully from the boxes so as not to damage the roots. Place them into the holes so the roots are on the bottom and the tips are just above the ground. Water them in gently but do not fill holes with soil – the water will cause enough soil to settle around the roots. At each subsequent watering, more soil will fill in the holes and this will help blanch them which improves the flavour and texture. As the plants grow, keep ridging up soil to just below the growing point to continue the blanching process. Feed young plants fortnightly with LAN at a rate of 40 g per metre row, or use a high nitrogen liquid feed. Small, frequent feedings and regular watering will give the best results. Leeks take up to 20 weeks before they mature, but you can start lifting some out as soon as the stems are about 1-2 cm in diameter. The leeks must be lifted carefully. Loosen the soil with a fork and then lift out with a trowel – do not pull them out.

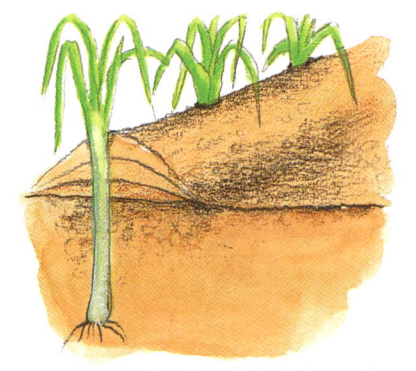

Ridged up soil helps keep the leek shoots white.

Leeks at a glance

Type of vegetable: Stem; cool season.
Edible parts: Stems.
Best soil: Rich, well dug; pH 6,5-7.
When to plant: Late summer to autumn.
The right amount: 1 or 2 x 1,5 m rows.
How to plant: Sow in seed boxes; transplant into individual holes 15 cm apart with 35 cm between rows.
Care: Feed and water regularly.
When to harvest: 11-20 weeks after planting, depending on the season.
How to harvest: Carefully loosen soil around plants and gently lift them out.
Successive plantings: Every 8 weeks during sowing season.
Storage methods: Refrigerate or blanch and freeze.

Possible problems

Leeks are remarkably problem free.

Seedlings collapse just after planting
Cause: Cutworm
Place cardboard collars around plants at planting time or dig in a cutworm bait.

Recommended cultivars

Giant Italian
Carentan

Helpful hints
◆ To stop soil from falling into leaf sheaths when ridging up, put tall, stiff cardboard collars around the plants.
◆ To clean leeks after lifting, take off the thin roots, cut the leaves about 15 cm above the white stem, cut the stem lengthwise and wash in plenty of water to remove any soil particles.

LETTUCE

One of the most widely grown of all salad vegetables, lettuces are available in a variety of types. While the crisphead lettuce is commercially grown in large quantities, the other types, especially the loose-leaf lettuce, are becoming increasingly popular in the home garden. Loose-leaf lettuces are attractive looking plants which can be grown as an edging to a mixed border and, along with the various other kinds, also grow very well in containers.

TYPES OF LETTUCE

Crisphead lettuces form firm, solid heads with large, crisp, pale-green to almost white leaves. They do best in cooler conditions but there are selected cultivars available which are bred to tolerate heat.

Butterhead lettuces form smaller heads than crispheads. The leaves are also thicker and more loosely folded to form a rather rose-like open head. The leaves, which are more delicate than crisphead lettuce leaves, have a smoother texture and are a distinctive creamy yellow-green colour. The outer leaves of butterhead lettuces can be used until the inner head has formed.

Loose-leaf lettuces are also known as 'cut-and-come-again' lettuces as they do not form a solid head but grow until the plant begins to flower. This means that the leaves can be picked for salads and for garnishing over a long period. Loose-leaf lettuce is also easier to grow than the other types, being less susceptible to changes in weather conditions. There are a number of different varieties of loose-leaf lettuce, including both green and red coloured ones with oak leaf shaped leaves as well as frilly leaves or ruffled leaves.

Cos lettuce has a very upright growth habit and forms a long head with narrow leaves, which are delicate and damage easily. Not well known or widely grown, cos lettuces have a particularly sweet flavour but they need cool growing conditions.

This selection of lettuce shows the wide range which can be grown.

GROWING LETTUCES

Lettuces can be grown almost throughout the year with June and July being the least favourable months. For the best results, all types of lettuce must grow quickly and suffer no setbacks. The plants have a shallow root system and need excellent drainage or they may be subject to bottom rot. Prepare the soil well by digging plenty of compost and well-rotted manure into the top 15-20 cm of soil. Use a dressing of 2.3.2 at the rate of 100 g per m² as a pre-planting fertilizer.

The seed can be sown directly into the bed and then thinned to the required distances, or it can be sown into seed boxes. As only a few plants are needed at frequent intervals, buying transplants is often more practical. Improved hybrid lettuces, especially fancy loose-leaf cultivars, are often only available as commercially bought transplants.

The seedlings should be set out into the beds once they are about 10 cm high. Planting distances will depend on the type – crispheads and butterheads should be planted 30 cm apart, and cos and loose-leaf lettuces about 25 cm apart. Young lettuce seedlings break very easily and so great care must be taken when setting out the plants and firming them into the ground. They must also be watered in gently, either with a fine sprinkling system or a watering can. Do not plant seedlings of the heading lettuces deeper than they were in the seed trays or they may not form good heads. As lettuces flop easily after planting, especially in hot weather, transplanting them in the late afternoon lessens transplanting stress. Mulching

A simple frame covered with shade cloth will protect lettuces from the heat.

the soil around young lettuce plants will help keep the soil moist and cool. In very hot weather and in hot, dry areas, lettuces will benefit from being lightly shaded, 30% shade cloth being the most appropriate. Shading also helps to stop the plants running to flower too fast.

The plants will need plenty of water – every day in summer if the conditions are very hot and dry, as a lack of water can result in bitter leaves. After 3-4 weeks, feed the plants with a high nitrogen fertilizer, such as LAN or an enriched organic product, and repeat 3 weeks later. As crisphead lettuces begin to make firm heads, reduce watering slightly to avoid bottom rot.

Crisphead, butterhead and cos lettuces should be ready 7-10 weeks after transplanting, depending on the weather, while you should be able to start picking the leaves of loose-leaf lettuce about 5-7 weeks after transplanting. Either pull up the whole plant to harvest crisphead, butterhead and cos lettuces and break off the roots, or cut the plant off at ground level with a sharp knife. Do not leave crisphead lettuce too long in the ground once the heads are firm in the hope of getting bigger heads – there is a real danger of the plants rotting in the centre or at ground level.

Possible problems

Seedlings fall over and wilt
Cause: Cutworm
Put cardboard collars around plants or use cutworm bait.

Leaves become distorted, small insects on undersides
Cause: Aphids
Spray with soapy water or a herbal spray; use a suitable insecticide; take careful note of withholding period.

Heads are slimy and rotten when picked
Cause: Bottom rot
Pick heads as soon as they are big enough to use; spray soil around plants with suitable soil fungicide. Problem worse in hot humid conditions.

Plants go to seed before making heads
Cause: Incorrect cultivars for the season; poor preparation of the soil and insufficient nutrition

Recommended cultivars

Always ensure you plant the right cultivars and make sure plants are kept well fed and watered. Cultivars grown out of season will quickly turn to seed.

Crisphead
Spring heading – sow July to September
Commander
El Toro
Great Lakes
New York
Robinvale

Lettuce at a glance

Type of plant: Leafy; intermediate.
Edible parts: Leaves and stems.
Best soil: Rich, moisture-retaining; ph 6,5-7.
When to plant: Almost all year, depending on cultivars.
The right amount: 4-6 plants per transplanting or depending on requirements.
How to plant: Sow seed into furrows or seed boxes; transplant crisphead and butterhead lettuces 30 cm apart; loose-leaf and cos 25 cm apart.
Care: Regular watering; side-dressing of nitrogen.
When to harvest: 5-10 weeks depending on the cultivar and time of year.
How to harvest: Crispheads – once head is firm to the touch; butterheads and cos – once head has formed; loose-leaf – once leaves are of usable size.
Successive plantings: Crispheads and butterheads every 2-3 weeks. Loose-leaf lettuces about every 4-6 weeks.
Storage: Refrigerate.

Summer heading – sow October to December
Commander
Great Lakes
King Crown
Robinvale

Autumn heading – sow January to March
Commander
El Toro
Great Lakes
Iceberg
New York

Winter heading – sow April to June
El Toro
Iceberg
Queen Crown
Wintercrisp
Valtemp

Butterhead lettuce
All The Year Round
Buttercrunch
Big Boston
Mammoth Butter
Note: Special cultivars, such as Citation, Floresta and Kragraner Sommer, are available directly from seed merchants.

Loose-leaf lettuce
Grand Rapids
Note: Special new cultivars are available directly from seed merchants, e.g. Lolla Rossa (curly red), Lollo Bionda (curly green), Carthago (green oak leaf), Salad Bowl (red oak leaf).

Lettuces are basically cool season crops, although there are now many cultivars which are suitable for warmer conditions. However, poor germination can occur if the soil temperature is more than 25 °C for butterheads and between 28-30 °C for crispheads. Keep the soil in the boxes moist to keep them cool. Better results are usually obtained when the seed is sown in the cool evening rather than in the morning.

Vegetables

Growing climbing, edible podded peas saves space in the small home garden.

PEAS

Peas are among the most widely grown vegetables in the temperate parts of the world. There are two main types of home garden peas – the common shelled peas and the less well-known edible podded peas which are eaten like green beans.

Shelled peas are grown commercially in enormous quantities for freezing and canning, while edible podded peas are becoming increasingly popular. They are mainly marketed fresh but are also being used for freezing purposes.

TYPES OF PEAS

Garden or shelled peas, also known as English peas, are the vegetables referred to in old books and nursery rhymes as 'pease'. With their sweet, nutritious, round seeds, they have been a favourite table vegetable since the 16th century. They grow on a sprawling vine and their white flowers are followed by the typical swollen pods.

Edible peas, also called snow peas, sugar peas or mangetout, are grown for their sweet, crunchy pods. There are both bush and tall-growing cultivars and these peas make excellent garden crops.

GROWING PEAS

Peas are essentially a cool season crop and give the best results when sown from autumn to early spring. As they can be badly affected by frost, they should be sown late in the season in areas where severe frost occurs, i.e. from July to August, while in the subtropical regions they do best when sown from late autumn to mid-winter.

Peas need a well-prepared soil, rich in organic matter such as compost and old, well-rotted manure. The soil can be improved with a light dressing of 2.3.2 at the rate of 60-75 g per m². As peas prefer neutral to slightly alkaline soils (pH 6-7,5), very acid soils should be limed well in advance to correct the pH levels. Do not use fresh manures or high nitrogen fertilizers as this will promote

Bush peas can be supported with twiggy sticks.

Bush peas grown between a frame of wire or string will prevent them from falling over.

Climbing peas will cling to a wire fence, trallis or a special pea net.

Peas at a glance

Type of plant: Seed-bearing vine; cool season.
Edible parts: Harvested seeds or entire pods of some types.
Best soil: Rich, very well drained; pH 6-7,5.
When to plant: Autumn to early spring.
The right amount: 1-3 m row for climbing types; 3-5 m row for bush types.
How to plant: Sow seed into furrows 3-5 cm apart with about 30-60 cm between rows.
Care: Keep soil damp; mulch; liquid feed once flowers form.
When to harvest: 2-2½ months from sowing for edible pods; 3-3½ months from sowing for shelled peas.
How to harvest: Carefully hand-pick pods.
Successive plantings: Every 2-3 weeks, depending on time and space.
Storage: Refrigerate or freeze.

plant growth at the expense of flowers and pods. The seed should be sown directly into the well-prepared soil – make sure that you work the soil over thoroughly, breaking it up into a fine tilth before watering well. Make a shallow furrow about 4 cm deep across the bed. Drop the seed in about 3-5 cm apart, cover with soil and firm down gently. Allow approximately 20-60 cm between rows, depending on whether the plants are supported or not.

While bush peas do not have to be staked they are easier to care for and harvest in the home garden if they are allowed to grow up twiggy sticks or small branches. Tall-growing edible pod peas must be grown up a fence or trellis which should be up to 2,5 m high.

Provided that the soil is damp at sowing time, it should not need watering until the seed germinates – over-watering at this stage can cause rotting. Carefully remove any weeds which appear as peas hate competition. Once the seedlings are about 5 cm high, draw some soil around them to give extra support and mulch the soil with compost or old grass clippings to retain soil moisture and to smother weed growth. Keep the soil damp at all times but not over-saturated.

If the soil has been well prepared, peas should not need extra feeding but a high potassium liquid fertilizer once they begin to flower will promote growth and prolong the harvesting period.

Peas should be ready for harvesting from 2½-3½ months after sowing, depending on the weather conditions and the cultivars – edible podded peas are ready earlier than shelled peas. Start picking the pods of shelled peas once they are plump and the seeds are well-formed. Do not let them get big and hard or slightly wrinkled as they will have a poor flavour. When pods are left too long on the plants, it discourages new flowers.

Edible podded peas should be picked when the pod is only slightly developed. For the best results, pick your peas at least twice a week. As the plants are very brittle, you should be extremely careful when picking the pods.

Possible problems

White deposits on leaves
Cause: Powdery mildew
Keep foliage as dry as possible; use a suitable fungicide.

Seed fails to germinate
Cause: Birds which eat seed
Cover newly sown seed with wire netting or crisscross beds with strands of black cotton.

Pods damaged
Cause: Birds
Protect the plants with a frame of light bird netting.

Holes in pods
Cause: American bollworm
Use a herbal spray or a suitable insecticide for chewing insects; take careful note of withholding period.

Holes in leaves
Cause: Snails and slugs
Use natural control methods or a recommended snail bait.

Leaves discolour and fall off
Cause: Red spider mite
Increase humidity around plants by spraying undersides of leaves, or use a suitable insecticide for sucking insects; take careful note of withholding period.

Peas are extremely fragile – hand-pick pods very carefully.

Recommended cultivars

Shelled peas:
Robert (early)
Greenfeast (medium)
Onward (late)

Edible pods:
Sugar Daddy (tall)
Sugar Snap (bush)

PEPPERS

Although commonly called peppers, these plants are not related to true pepper, which is one of the world's most common seasonings, but belong to the same family as tomatoes, eggplants and potatoes. There are two main types available – bell or sweet peppers, and hot or chilli peppers.

TYPES OF PEPPER

Bell peppers, because they are green initially, are often called green peppers and are sold by that name. They produce chunky, bell-shaped, sweet-flavoured fruits which usually turn red when mature, but there are cultivars which turn shades of yellow. Raw green or immature peppers contain Vitamin C but if allowed to mature fully on the plants, the peppers have a higher Vitamin C content, as well as Vitamin A, and a much sweeter flavour. The fruits are used in salads and can be stuffed and cooked or made into pickles. Commercially grown peppers are also dried and made into paprika.

Hot peppers (chillies) are also green when young but turn bright yellow or red when mature. They produce long slim pods and, once their seeds have been removed, are usually used dry and added to curries and other spicy dishes. Crushed hot peppers are a vital ingredient in curry powder and cayenne pepper is made from these varieties.

GROWING PEPPERS

Peppers need warm conditions and have a relatively short sowing season in most parts of the country, namely from August to November, although they can be sown almost all year round in subtropical areas. Peppers are best sown in protected seed boxes and then transplanted into the garden once the soil is warmer. As so few plants are needed and the seedlings are slow to develop, it is often more practical to buy seedlings as soon as they are available.

For the best results, peppers must grow quickly. Prepare the soil with plenty of compost and old manure plus a dressing of 2.3.2 about 100 g per m^2. Plant out sturdy young seedlings about 40-50 cm apart, slightly deeper than they were in their seed boxes. If the weather is very hot when the plants are set out, shade them with shade cloth, leafy twigs or shade caps. Keep the plants well watered and never allow them to dry even slightly.

Once they start to flower, feed with a small quantity of high potassium fertilizer such as 30 g of 3.1.5, or a suitable liquid fertilizer; repeat every 4-5 weeks. Pick the fruit as soon as it is big enough to use. Cut it off with a sharp knife, taking care not to break any branches. Do not let any fruit stay on the plant until it is old and wrinkled as this will inhibit the production of more flowers. As the plants are brittle and damage easily, they should be well staked in windy areas.

Poor flower set and dropped buds can be a problem, especially during hot, dry weather. Keeping the plants well mulched and regularly watered, as well as spraying the foliage during very dry conditions, should solve this problem. If the plants are well cared for and if the fruit is picked regularly, peppers will continue producing fruit for many months – it is only the start of the cold weather that stops them blooming.

New pepper cultivars come in a wide range of attractive colours and shapes.

Peppers are brittle plants – pick fruit carefully.

Possible problems

Leaves distorted and wrinkled
Cause: Aphids
Spray with soapy water; use a herbal spray or a suitable insecticide for sucking insects; take careful note of withholding period.

Lack of flowers
Cause: Excessive heat and dry conditions
Keep plants well watered and mulched – spray foliage lightly with water.

White deposit on foliage
Cause: Powdery mildew
Usually worse under hot, humid, damp conditions or too much shade. Avoid watering foliage and spray with suitable fungicide if very severe.

Recommended cultivars

Bell or sweet peppers
Californian Wonder (sweet)
Cayenne Long Slim (hot)
Florida Resistant Giant (sweet)
Lady Bell (F1 Hybrid) (sweet)

Peppers at a glance

Type of plant: Fleshy fruit; warm season.
Edible parts: Fruits.
Best soil: Fertile, well drained; pH 5,5-6,5.
When to plant: Late winter to early summer.
The right amount: 4-6 plants.
How to plant: Seed sown in seed trays; transplants into individual holes 40-50 cm apart.
Care: Regular watering and feeding; remember to spray foliage in hot weather to prevent petal drop.
When to harvest: From 11 weeks after transplanting.
How to harvest: Cut fruit carefully off plant with a sharp knife.
Successive plantings: 4-6 weeks, depending on weather.
Storage: Refrigerate or freeze

VEGETARIAN STUFFED PEPPERS

2 red or green peppers
30 g butter
30 g flour
425 ml milk
450 g cooked cauliflower
50 g breadcrumbs
salt and pepper to taste
pinch ground nutmeg

Cut off a thin slice from the stem ends of the peppers and remove the seeds. Parboil for 2 minutes in lightly salted water. Drain well.
   Make a white sauce by melting the butter in a saucepan. Stir in the flour and gradually add the milk, stirring constantly until smooth.
   Mash the cauliflower with the white sauce and add breadcrumbs, reserving some for garnish. Season with salt, pepper and nutmeg.
   Fill peppers to the top with the mixture, cover with breadcrumbs and dot with butter. Place in a buttered ovenproof dish. Preheat oven to 220 °C and place dish in oven to heat through. Lastly, grill quickly until brown and crisp.
SERVES 2

POTATOES

Although potatoes are one of the most widely used food crops and are commercially grown in huge quantities, they are not an ideal home garden vegetable. The main reason is that they are in the ground for up to and over 20 weeks and they also need a considerable amount of space. They are also subject to a number of serious fungal diseases.
   Nevertheless, while it is not practical in the home garden to produce large amounts of potatoes for storage, nothing beats the flavour of freshly dug baby potatoes and so some space should be found for just a few plants.

Growing potatoes

While potatoes are frost-sensitive and dislike cold conditions, they also do not thrive under excessive heat. The worst planting months are usually November and December and often the best results in the home garden are obtained from spring and autumn plantings, depending on climatic conditions.

As potatoes can suffer from a variety of serious fungal and viral diseases, it is of the utmost importance to buy certified seed and not use old kitchen potatoes which have started to sprout.

Seed potatoes are specially grown tubers and are usually the size of a large egg. Tubers, which are made to sprout before planting, usually make stronger plants. To sprout the tubers, put them in boxes of damp soil – you can even use cardboard egg boxes and keep them in a cool, shady place. When they have developed short, strong shoots, they are ready for planting.

The soil for potatoes must be very well prepared by initially digging over the soil to at least a spade's depth and removing any old weeds, stones and hard clods of soil. Try to obtain a loose, crumbly texture. If only a few plants are to be grown, mark out a trench about 15 cm wide x 15 cm deep. Spread a 5 cm layer of compost over and a dressing of 2.3.4 fertilizer at the rate of 50-75 g per metre row along the bottom of the trench. Partly fill in the trench with topsoil. Then set out the sprouted tubers along the trench about 20-25 cm apart and cover with soil. If planting more than one row, there should be 75 cm between the rows. Remember potatoes have wide top growth and need space. Once the shoots have emerged through the soil and are about 30 cm high, draw soil up around them to form a ridge or hill. This helps support the plants and protects the tubers from heat and caterpillars. Keep ridging up the soil as this also encourages the development of more tubers.

POTATOES AT A GLANCE

Type of plant: Tuber; warm season or cool season.
Edible parts: Tuber.
Best soil: Fertile, well-drained soil; pH 5-6,5.
When to plant: Autumn/spring or depending on climate.
The right amount: 4-6 plants.
How to plant: Plant individual sprouted tubers.
Care: Regular watering and ridging of soil.
When to harvest: 3-4 weeks after flowering – about 3 months after planting.
How to harvest: Dig out tubers gently.
Successive plantings: Depends on climatic conditions.
Storage: Best eaten fresh.

Home-grown baby potatoes have an unbeatable flavour.

POTATO SALAD

500 g small to medium potatoes
3-4 tbsp prepared French dressing
salt and pepper
125 ml thick mayonnaise
30 ml fresh cream
pinch paprika
slices of pickled walnuts

Scrub potatoes well and boil in their skins for about 15 minutes. Do not overcook or they will break up when sliced and tossed in dressing.

Peel while still hot and cut into slices. Place in a bowl and add French dressing immediately so that it is absorbed by the potatoes. Season, cover bowl and chill in the fridge. When ready to serve, mix in one tablespoon of mayonnaise and turn the potatoes into a serving dish. Dilute remaining mayonnaise to coating consistency with cream and spoon over salad. Dust with paprika and garnish with slices of pickled walnuts.
SERVES 4-6

Hints:
- To stop potatoes from going black when they have been boiled, add a little vinegar to the water.
- Baby potatoes should only be scraped or brushed before cooking. If you cannot cook them immediately, keep them under water to prevent discoloration but do not leave longer than overnight.

Always keep the plants well watered but where fungal diseases are a problem, avoid wetting foliage in the late afternoon. Use the furrows alongside the plants as irrigation channels. If the soil has been well prepared initially, extra feeding should not be necessary.

Baby or new potatoes should be ready to harvest about 3-4 weeks after the plants have flowered and as soon as the foliage begins to go yellow. Always check your crop by carefully digging soil away from the ridge; if the potatoes are about the size of a medium-sized hen's egg, start taking them out. Loosen the soil with a fork along the sides of the ridges and carefully lift out the tubers.

Possible problems

Leaves reduced to lacy holes and flowers eaten
Cause: Leaf beetles, e.g. potato ladybirds
Spray with herbal spray or use a suitable insecticide for chewing insects.

Tubers full of holes and are therefore inedible
Cause: Tuber moth larvae
Protect tubers by keeping soil well ridged up against the plants.

Leaves develop black marks with yellow outer rings
Cause: Late blight
Difficult to control; try to keep foliage as dry as possible; spray with a suitable fungicide as a preventative measure as soon as shoots develop. Immediately pull out and burn infected plants at the first sign of disease. Only plant certified tubers. Avoid planting potatoes in ground previously occupied by as tomatoes or again in the same place as any previously infected potato plants.

Recommended cultivars

BP 1
Up-to-Date
Van der Plank

Note: As climatic conditions play an important role when growing potatoes, always check with local experts or your local nursery as to which are the best cultivars suitable for growing in your particular area.

Ridging up soil around the plants stops the 'greening' of tubers and protects them from tuber moth.

Swiss Chard Spinach

While there are a number of types of spinach (such as Chinese and New Zealand spinach) and spinach-like plants, the easiest and most rewarding for the home gardener is Swiss chard spinach, often referred to as spinach beet. This plant is actually a type of beetroot which produces large, crinkly, spinach-like leaves. True spinach belongs to a different family and while it produces very fine quality leaves, it requires cool conditions to prevent it running too quickly to seed.

Growing Swiss chard spinach

Swiss chard spinach can be grown almost throughout the year, but in cold areas May, June and July are the least favourable sowing months. About 12-15 plants will be sufficient per planting, with about 3-4 months between plantings, depending on weather conditions. As the plants grow and produce over a long period, it is important to prepare the soil really well. Dig as much compost and well-rotted manure into the bed as possible, then work in a pre-planting fertilizer, such as 2.3.2, at the rate of about 60 g per m^2, or use an enriched organic product.

Swiss chard spinach grows easily from seed sown directly into the vegetable beds. You can also plant out young seedlings, however, either raised yourself in seed boxes or bought from a nursery.

Before sowing seed, rake the soil over well to break up any lumps and to ensure a good tilth. Make shallow furrows across the bed, about 40 cm apart. As the seed is large and easy to handle, sow the individual seeds about 8-10 cm apart along the rows. Fill in the furrows with soil, firm it down and water lightly. Keep the soil damp and, in very hot conditions, use a light mulch to help keep the soil cool and damp.

Once the seed has germinated, it should be thinned out to give each one enough space to develop. Carefully pull out the smaller, weaker plants so that you are left with strong, sturdy plants spaced about 20 cm apart. The thinnings can be used to fill in any gaps between the rows.

To ensure that the plants grow quite quickly, keep them regularly watered and give them a light dressing of LAN or 3.2.1 fertilizer at the rate of 50 g per metre row. Always water fertilizer in well. Repeat about a month later. You could also feed the plants with a side-dressing of an enriched organic product. Feeding the plants with a liquid manure solution or a commercial liquid fertilizer every 3-4 weeks is also very beneficial and helps promote the production of plenty of new leaves.

The leaves can be picked once they are large enough – usually approximately 8-10 weeks after sowing or 6-8 weeks after transplanting. Pick the largest outer leaves by giving them a sharp downward twist. Always leave about 4-5 leaves on each plant and about 7-10 days between picking.

You should be able to harvest leaves for about 3-4 months and even longer, but once the plants start to produce flowers, they quickly deteriorate and should be dug out.

Both the spinach stalks and the leaves can be used raw or as a cooked vegetable.

Swiss chard spinach at a glance

Type of vegetable: Leafy; intermediate.
Edible parts: Leaves and stalks.
Best soil: Very well prepared; pH 6-7.
When to plant: Almost all year; June and July least favourable.
The right amount: 12-15 plants per planting.
How to plant: Sow seed directly into soil; thin to 20 cm apart.
Care: Water regularly; feed every 4-6 weeks; mulch in hot weather.
When to harvest: Once leaves are large enough; pick every 7-10 days.
How to harvest: Cut off leaves with a sharp knife.
Successive plantings: Every 4-6 weeks, depending on space.
Storage: Refrigerate or freeze.

Possible problems

A very easy crop with no major pests or diseases. Always wash well before cooking as leaves can get very dirty and snails tend to cling to them.

Holes in leaves
Cause: Caterpillars or slugs and snails
Hand-pick or use a herbal spray; use snail bait.

Brown marks on leaves, which then turn gray and rot
Cause: Leaf spot fungal disease
Avoid overhead watering; spray with suitable fungicide; problem worst in hot humid conditions.

Recommended cultivars

Fordhook Giant
Lucullus

SPINACH SOUFFLE

750 g spinach, parboiled and minced
250 ml white sauce (see page 56)
3 eggs, separated
250 ml Cheddar cheese, grated
a pinch grated nutmeg
salt and pepper to taste

Mix the spinach with the white sauce. Beat the egg yolks and add to spinach mixture along with the cheese and seasoning. Beat the egg whites and fold them into the mixture. The mixture should be thick and creamy.
   Bake in a greased ovenproof dish at 180 °C for about 40 minutes.
SERVES 4

Although Swiss chard spinach is extremely easy to grow, if you do not have success, it could be due to acid soil. Test the soil and if below 5,5 on the pH scale, treat with dolomitic lime well in advance of planting.

Rows of vegetables share this small space with roses and ground cover erigeron.

TOMATOES

Of all the vegetables, nothing can beat home-grown tomatoes, especially when you compare their taste to commercially grown ones. The reason for this is that home-grown tomatoes are allowed to colour fully and develop their flavour before being picked, while commercially grown tomatoes are picked green. Tomatoes are ideal container plants and grow well in pots.

Types of tomato

Apart from the size and shape of their fruit, tomatoes are divided into two distinct types on account of growth habit, namely determinate and indeterminate tomatoes.

The more commonly cultivated determinate cultivars are often of American origin. Once they have grown to approximately 1-1,2 m high, the top shoot forms flowers as do the side shoots. Indeterminate types will go on growing taller until the top growing point is pinched out as well as the side shoots. Indeterminate tomatoes should always be tied up long tall stakes up to 2,5 m high and are best pruned to only one to two stems with all the side growths removed.

Determinate tomatoes usually have larger fruits and mature quicker than indeterminate tomatoes but the latter go on fruiting for a longer period.

The taste of home-grown, sun-ripened tomatoes is sweet and fruity.

However, staked and pruned indeterminate tomatoes need careful feeding and care if they are to grow well. As well as garden use, they are suited to tunnel and shade house cultivation.

Growing tomatoes

Tomatoes are essentially a warm season crop and cannot tolerate even a few degrees of frost. Cold weather will also slow down their growth so the first sowings of the season can only be made in spring, once the weather warms up. The main sowing times are therefore August to November in most parts of the country but late summer to winter in the warmer subtropical regions. To ensure early crops, however, seed can be sown in late winter and early spring in sheltered seed boxes and the plants transplanted once the weather improves.

As only a few plants (about two to four plants) are needed at a time, it is often more practical to buy transplants.

Tomatoes are greedy, quick-growing plants which must have a very rich organic soil. When preparing the soil for only a few plants, dig large, individual holes about 45 cm square and 45 cm deep. The holes should be approximately 70 cm -1 m apart. If the plants are to be staked, which is always advisable, put in the supports at the same time as digging the holes. Put a dressing of about 30 g of 2.3.2 fertilizer right at the bottom of the hole and fill in the hole with a rich mixture of soil, compost and well-rotted manure. Water well and allow to settle.

Determinate tomato varieties (left) tend to be more popular than indeterminate types (right) as they usually have larger fruit and mature quicker.

Unlike other vegetables, tomatoes benefit from several transplantings before being finally set out in the garden. If you grow your own seedlings, transplant them into small pots as soon as they reach seed leaf stage, setting the seedlings into the soil slightly deeper than they were in the seed box with the soil level just below the leaves. Once they have developed about 4-6 true leaves, transplant them again into bigger pots, also setting them deeper than they were before. This transplanting can be repeated twice or three times, depending on the rate of growth. The tomatoes are ready to be planted out once they are about 25 cm tall and the first flower bud has started to form.

Plant the young tomatoes in the prepared hole, digging out a hole just slightly bigger than the plant's rootball. Firm down well and water in carefully. If staking with a single stake, the young plant must be placed as close as possible to it and immediately tied lightly to it.

Tomatoes must grow steadily and suffer no setbacks if they are to produce healthy crops. They must be kept well and deeply watered at all times, about every 7-10 days while the weather is cool but as much as every 3-4 days once it warms up, especially in hot, dry conditions. Mulching the plants with compost or any other suitable organic material will help keep the soil damp.

As the plants are highly susceptible to fungal diseases, they should never be watered overhead but rather surface irrigated. Drawing up soil around the individual plants to form a wide, shallow water basin is an excellent method to use in the home garden. Because of the problem of fungal diseases, as well as certain insect pests, it is advisable to follow a preventative spraying programme from the time the plants are first set out in the garden.

Feed the plants with about 15 g of 3.1.5 fertilizer per plant, or an enriched organic product as soon as they start to set fruit; continue to feed them every 3-4 weeks. The plants can be fed with a liquid feed if preferred.

Home-grown tomatoes are ready to pick once they are fully coloured and firm to the touch. Don't let the fruit stay on the plant too long or it will become over-ripe. If you need to spray the plants with insecticides or fungicides, pick all fruit which is slightly coloured and allow to ripen indoors.

Tomatoes at a glance

Type of vegetable: Fleshy fruit, warm season.
Edible part: Fruit.
Best soil: Very well prepared; pH 5,5-6,5.
When to plant: Spring to late summer; winter in warm areas.
The right amount: 2-4 plants.
How to plant: Seed sown in seed trays; transplant into individual holes 70 cm - 1 m apart.
Care: Regular watering and feeding.
When to harvest: From about 9-13 weeks from transplanting, depending on cultivar.
How to harvest: Pick fruit by hand.
Successive plantings: Every 4 weeks, depending on climatic conditions.
Storage: Refrigerate or make into a purée for freezing.

For blemish-free tomatoes, regular spraying is necessary.

Possible problems

Tomatoes are unfortunately subject to a number of pests, but are more seriously affected by fungal and bacterial diseases. It is therefore of the utmost importance to choose the best and most disease-resistant tomato cultivars suited to your growing region, to water and feed the plants correctly, to practise crop rotation and to follow a regular spraying programme to protect the plants from possible fungal diseases.

Leaves distorted and yellow; plenty of small white flying insects on undersides
Cause: White fly
Spray with soapy water or herbal spray or use a suitable insecticide for sucking insects – thoroughly wet the undersides of the leaves. Try to spray early in the morning, if possible.

How to stake tomatoes

Although tomatoes do not have to be staked, staking promotes healthier growth, unblemished fruit and larger crops. There are a number of ways of staking plants, depending on the type of plant. One of the most popular methods is to tie the plant up a stout stake. The stake should be about 1,5-2 m long so that it can be driven deep into the soil. You can also support the plants by planting each one within a square or triangle of stakes and then tying wire at intervals around the stakes. Sturdy wire mesh can also be used to make a 'cage' for the tomatoes and ready-made tomato cages are available in some centres. If using wire mesh, the holes must be just large enough for you to put your hands through to pick the fruit.

Tomato 'cage'

Single staking

Fruit has holes in it with a green worm in the fruit
Cause: American bollworm or plusia looper caterpillar
Spray with herbal spray or use a suitable insecticide for chewing insects – take careful note of withholding period.

Leaves go yellowish, turn brown and drop off
Cause: Red spider mite
Worse in hot dry weather – spray undersides of leaves with water early in the morning in hot dry weather; use a soapy water solution or a herbal spray; use a suitable miticide and take careful note of withholding period.

Leaves develop brown or black spots with target-like rings and the fruit is damaged
Cause: Early blight or target spot
Spray plants with a suitable fungicide – take note of withholding period; only surface irrigate plants; pick up and destroy all diseased leaves and fruits.

Leaves become blotchy and brown, then black with discoloured fruit
Cause: Late blight
Spray with suitable fungicide – note withholding period; surface irrigate; pick up and destroy all diseased leaves and fruit.

Fruit malformed or misshapen
Cause: Catface – physiological problem due to poor pollination brought on by sudden cold weather, incorrect fertilization or overhead irrigation

Fruit goes black and rots at the top
Cause: Blossom end rot, a physiological problem caused mainly by incorrect or irregular watering as well as a lack of calcium, especially on acid soils

Recommended cultivars

Bite Size (cocktail tomato) – indeterminate
Flora Dade – determinate
FMX 785 – determinate
Heinz 1370 – determinate
Karina – determinate
Manapal – indeterminate
Moneymaker – indeterminate
Rodade – semi-indeterminate
Sixpak – indeterminate

Note: A number of other excellent modern cultivars are available directly from the seed merchants and also in seedling form from nurseries.

Keep young tomato plants upright by firming the soil down well around them when planting.

Easy-to-grow turnips are a must for the winter garden.

TURNIPS

Turnips are among the easiest of the root vegetables to grow and can be relied upon to provide quick-maturing crops through the cooler months of the year. While they are grown primarily for their round, tasty roots, the young leaves can be cooked like spinach.

Growing turnips

Although basically best as a cool season crop which is sown from late summer to autumn, turnips can be grown almost throughout the year with mid-winter being the least favourable sowing time, except in the subtropical regions.

Like most root vegetables, turnips need a very well-worked, friable soil if they are to make well-shaped roots. They make a good follow-on crop to heavy feeders such as tomatoes. Dig the sowing area over and add extra compost if necessary. Then work in a light dressing of pre-planting fertilizer such as 2.3.2 at the rate of 40-60 g per m², or use an enriched organic product. As the plants do better in a fairly firm soil, lightly tread down the sowing area. Mark out shallow furrows across the bed, 1 cm deep and about 25-30 apart.

One to two rows of 1-1,5 m per sowing should provide plenty of turnips, with successive sowings every 3-4 weeks, depending on space. Sow the fine seed as thinly as possible, then cover with soil and water in gently. If the weather is still warm, cover with a fine mulch to help conserve soil moisture. Turnips germinate quickly – usually in about 3-10 days. After 2 weeks, if the seedlings are very close together, thin them out so that they are about 5-7 cm apart. A second thinning should be carried out about 2-3 weeks later if necessary.

Keep the plants regularly watered – any sudden lack of water will spoil the texture of the roots. Although they should not need extra feeding if the soil was prepared correctly, a light side-dressing of 25 g of 4.1.1 fertilizer per metre row, or a fairly high nitrogen liquid fertilizer, will encourage growth.

Turnips should be ready to harvest 8-10 weeks after sowing. To extend harvesting time, pull out individual ones as soon as they are ready to use. As the roots naturally push up slightly above the ground, it is easy to see how big they are. Do not leave in for too long or they will be coarse and stringy.

Possible problems

Young leaves distorted and small insects noticeable
Cause: Aphids
Spray with soapy water or herbal spray; use a suitable insecticide formulated for sucking insects.

Leaves eaten
Cause: Caterpillars, especially white cabbage moth
Hand-pick if possible; spray with a herbal spray or use a suitable insecticide for sucking insects if severe infestation.

Poor quality roots with brown marks and cracks
Cause: Boron deficiency, usually only found on extremely alkaline or very recently limed soils
Try to work the soil to a pH of 6,5; watering young seedlings with a borax solution may help to save existing crops.

Recommended cultivars

Purple Top
White Globe

Turnips at a glance

Type of vegetable: Root; cool season.
Edible parts: Roots and leaves.
Best soil: Well worked, friable; pH level 6-7.
When to plant: Late summer to autumn.
The right amount: One to two x 1-1,5 m rows.
How to plant: Seed sown in furrows; 25-30 cm between rows.
Care: Regular watering; thin to 5-7 cm apart.
When to harvest: Once big enough to use – 8-10 weeks from sowing.
How to harvest: Loosen soil, pull out.
Successive plantings: Every 3-4 weeks.
Storage: Refrigerate with tops on.

OTHER VEGETABLES IN BRIEF

The following are vegetables which can also be grown in the small home garden but, with the exception of radish, soup celery and salad onions, are not always as easy or reliable to grow as the crops which I have already described.

BROAD BEANS

This is a cool season vegetable which should be sown during autumn and winter in most areas. It needs an extremely well-prepared, rich, organic, slightly acid soil. Sow double rows 75-90 cm apart with about 15-20 cm between the seeds. Keep well watered and feed twice with a high nitrogen fertilizer. They are ready to harvest from about 18 weeks. Black aphid can be a serious pest.
Recommended cultivar: Aquadulce

Radishes mature quicker than any other vegetable.

Brussels sprouts must always be picked from the bottom upwards.

BRUSSELS SPROUTS

This is a cool season crop with similar growing needs to broccoli. It should be sown from December to February for autumn transplanting. The soil must be well prepared with plenty of compost and a 2.3.4 pre-planting fertilizer. Plants must be kept well watered and given two high nitrogen feeds during the growing season. The first sprouts should be ready about 13-15 weeks after transplanting. Strip away lower leaves and start picking from the bottom upwards. Pests and diseases are the same which affect cabbage and broccoli.
Recommended cultivars: Atlantic and Long Island; best results from F1 hybrid seed such as Jade Cross

CELERY

To grow blanched celery successfully takes a great deal of care and attention. It is a cool season crop which needs continuous moisture and an extremely fertile soil. The seed should be sown in seed boxes and then transplanted to 30 cm apart.

To blanch the stems, paper, cardboard or black plastic is wrapped around the plants once they are well established. Blanched celery should be ready to cut about 20 weeks after transplanting. Soup or green celery, which is not blanched, is an easy to grow crop and only a few plants will provide enough leaves for soups or stews and small sticks for salads and casseroles.
Recommended cultivar: Golden Self-Blanching

ONIONS

Onions for dry bulb production are not a recommended crop for the small home garden as they take a long time to mature, from 5-7 months, depending on the cultivars. They also need an abundance of moisture during the initial growth period and different cultivars require different numbers of daylight hours to bulb successfully.

If you decide to grow onions, check with local experts as to which cultivars would do best in your region. Seed is sown into seed boxes and then transplanted into rows 30 cm apart with 25-40 cm between the plants. Onion transplants are usually available and onion sets (small bulbs) are also available in some centres.
Recommended cultivars: Australian Brown, Texas Grano, Caledon Globe

PARSNIPS

Although slow to mature, parsnips can be a useful crop, especially in winter. The main sowing period is autumn and spring and the soil should be prepared in the same way as carrots. The seed should be sown as thinly as possible and then thinned to 5-7 cm apart. The rows should be about 30 cm apart. The first roots should be ready about 16-20 weeks after sowing. As parsnips are slow to germinate and then to mature, the seed can be mixed with radish seed. The quick-growing radishes protect the weaker parsnip seeds, help keep the parsnips apart and will be out of the ground long before the parsnips need the space for root development.
Recommended cultivar: Hollow Crown

RADISHES

Radishes are not a major edible vegetable crop but are a popular ingredient for salads and as a garnish or decoration on certain savoury dishes. They are extremely easy to grow and are ready to harvest in about 3-5 weeks, depending on season and cultivar. They can be grown almost throughout the year with June and July being the least favourable sowing times. Although radishes grow in almost any soil, they do best on well-worked, friable soil similar to that needed by carrots and parsnips.
Recommended cultivars: Cherry Belle, Sparkler and Red King, amongst others

SPINACH

Not to be confused with the more widely grown Swiss chard spinach, this type, also known as true spinach, is only successful as a cool season crop and should be sown from March to April. It needs well-prepared, fertile soil and should be sown as thinly as possible in rows about 30 cm apart. The seed should be thinned out to 20-30 cm apart. The first leaves should be ready for picking after approximately 8-10 weeks after sowing.
Recommended cultivar: Viroflay

VEGETABLES WHICH NEED PLENTY OF SPACE

Where there is enough space, certain of the trailing vegetables can be successful, while home-grown, freshly picked sweetcorn has a flavour no bought sweetcorn can match.

SQUASH

Where space permits, a number of different types of the bush and trailing squash can be grown. These include butternut, custard, hubbard and gem squash, as well as the closely related pumpkin. Most have a long growing season and should be sown from spring to early summer. Squashes need a rich, well-composted and well-manured soil. The seed is sown directly into hills. The bush types should be 90 cm apart with the trailing types at least 1 m apart. Because of the problem of powdery mildew, the plants should be surface irrigated. Mulching the soil helps to conserve water. Pumpkin fly can be a major problem and bait must be applied as soon as the plants start to flower. Squash are ready to harvest after 8-20 weeks, depending on variety.
Recommended cultivars: Little Gem, Golden Hubbard, Green Hubbard

If you have the space, grow a variety of bush and trailing squash.

STUFFED HUBBARD SQUASH

1 young medium hubbard squash
2-3 onions, diced
500 ml table celery
500 g ripe skinned tomatoes, finely chopped
30 ml butter
salt and pepper

Cut the top off the squash, scrape out the pips and discard them. Boil the whole squash carefully in lightly salted boiling water. When just soft, remove from water, taking care not to break it. Drain well and keep warm.

Braise the vegetables gently in the butter until cooked. Season with salt and pepper. Fill the squash with the vegetable mixture and serve at once.
SERVES 4

For the best results, sweetcorn should be planted in short blocks to aid pollination.

SWEET MELONS

Usually thought of more as a fruit than a vegetable, melons belong to the same family as cucumbers, squash and marrows. Also known as spanspek or cantaloupe, they are a summer crop which needs a long, warm growing season and should be sown from spring to early summer. The seed should be sown into very well-composted and manured hills which are about 1 m apart. Because moisture is vital at all stages of growth, the plants should be mulched. The mulch will also help keep the fruit clean and reduce the possibility of rotting. To encourage plenty of flowers on the side shoots, the long trailers should be pinched back once they are about 70 cm long. Harvest after about 2½-3 months, depending on the cultivar. Fruit fly is a serious pest and bait must be regularly used to control it.
Recommended cultivar: Hales Best 36

SWEETCORN

Freshly picked sweetcorn has an outstanding flavour and as a home garden crop sweetcorn is well worthwhile, provided you have sufficient space. Because it is wind pollinated, sweetcorn should be sown in short blocks and not in long rows. Blocks of 3-4 rows about 1-2 m long give good results.

The seed should be sown from spring to mid-summer. Sow thinly within the rows with 15 cm between the seed, and then thin out to about 30 cm apart. Mulch the soil and then keep it moist by deep, regular soaking. Feed the plants with a high nitrogen fertilizer such as LAN at the rate of 30 g per metre row.

The cobs are usually ready to pick after about 9-12 weeks. The kernels should be full and exude a milky fluid when pricked. Do not leave the cobs on the plants for too long as they will deteriorate rapidly.
Recommended cultivars: Jubilee, Golden Bantam, Stowels Evergreen
Note: There are also a number of special F1 hybrid cultivars which are worth trying to obtain.

Various types of citrus are among the most rewarding of fruit trees to grow in the home garden.

THE FRUITFUL CHOICE

While there is a wide range of fruit-producing plants which can be grown in the home garden, first choice must go to those plants which yield the biggest crops for the least amount of effort, as well as those which can be used for jams, preserves and fruit juices or which can be bottled or frozen.

Local growing conditions, however, are a major factor contributing to success or failure. Subtropical fruit like pawpaws thrive in areas such as the Transvaal Lowveld and Natal coast. They can also be grown in cooler regions, even those with light frost, if planted in a warm, sheltered spot. However, they cannot be grown in cold, inland areas which experience moderate to severe frost. On the other hand, there are many fruit trees, particularly the deciduous types like apples and pears, which actually need cold winters if they are to bear well.

Rainfall and the availability of irrigation water must also be taken into account. Few will produce regular crops unless they can be kept well watered. The rainfall pattern also plays an important role – too much rain when a crop is ripening can cause fruit to split or swell. Fortunately, in many cases there are cultivars which have been developed to resist all these problems.

The prevalence and severity of fruit pests can be a limiting factor. For some varieties, such as deciduous fruits, the worst pests are fruit fly and codling moth. Again, if you choose early-bearing cultivars, the problem is easier to control. Another way of lessening the possible outbreaks of fruit fly is to avoid having trees, such as loquats, in the garden as these produce ideal overwintering conditions for fruit fly.

Always be sure that you have enough space for your fruit-producing plants. This applies in particular to the fruit trees and nut-bearing trees. Some are fairly compact and do not require a large amount of space but others like macadamias, mangoes and litchis are really only suited to very big gardens, not so much because of their height but because of their wide-spreading habit.

The way the tree is pollinated is another factor to be considered. While the majority of fruit trees are self-pollinating (that they don't need a pollinating partner to set their crops), others must be cross-pollinated. With cross-pollination you should therefore have two trees of the same type in your garden, or at least one very nearby, or the yield will be very poor. However, such trees might throw too much shade over small-growing plants.

WHERE TO PLANT

Practically all the fruiting plants, from trees, vines and creepers to cane berries and strawberries, need a sunny, open position which is protected from very strong winds.

When planting a tree which needs a warmer climate than your region's, plant it in a warm, sheltered position such as a north-facing corner. Where frost is a problem, try to ensure that the plant gets early morning shade so that the cells can thaw slowly.

The cool to cold climate types will prefer some afternoon shade in very hot areas and under dry conditions.

CLIMATE GUIDE

Temperate climate fruit –
7,5 °C-25 °C
Apples
Apricots
Berries
Citrus
Figs
Granadillas
Grapes
Guavas
Macadamias
Peaches and nectarines
Pears
Plums
Quinces
Strawberries

Subtropical fruit – 15 °C-27,5 °C
Avocados
Bananas*
Citrus
Figs
Litchis*
Mangoes*
Pawpaws
Pecans

Persimmons
Tree tomatoes
* need very warm, moist conditions

Cold climate fruit –10 °C-22,5 °C
Apples
Cherries
Pears
Quinces
Raspberries
Walnuts

Particularly prolific producers
Apricots
Citrus
Granadillas
Guavas
Pawpaws
Persimmons
Plums
Strawberries
Youngberries and boysenberries

Bought plants or home-grown?

While many fruit trees can be grown from pips, these take an extremely long time to grow to a worthwhile size and seldom, if ever, produce good crops. You can take cuttings of certain varieties but be sure to choose those known to be strong productive growers. Generally you will get the most reliable results from plants bought from reputable nurseries and garden centres.

The importance of cultivars

A factor often overlooked in the home garden is the choice of cultivars. Modern breeding methods have developed a wide range of cultivars of most of the popular types of fruit. When choosing one, make sure you know exactly which cultivar it is as certain cultivars grow better in certain areas. On the whole, you will find that local nurseries and garden centres stock the ones which do best in that area. The different cultivars also fruit at slightly different times so that if you have room for more than one peach tree, for example, you can extend the fruiting season by planting early, mid- and late season cultivars. The right cultivars are also important with trees which need cross-pollination. Certain cultivars make better cross-pollinating partners for other specific cultivars, as they flower at the optimum time.

While there are many cultivars available to the home gardener, you will not find all the commercial cultivars, particularly the apples and peaches which are bought in the shops. The main reason is that these have been bred for orchard conditions and intensive fruit farming methods and usually do not produce as well in the home garden.

The cultivars recommended under each entry are given merely as a guide. New cultivars are regularly introduced and you should seek advice from local growers on the best ones for your area.

Trees to be avoided

While loquat trees are fruit producers, the fruit has little use, although it can be eaten raw. Growers of fruit which are very susceptible to fruit fly (such as peaches) should avoid growing loquats in the garden. The fruit attracts fruit fly and the pest also overwinters in the rough bark and protective leaves of the loquat tree. In areas where fruit fly is very prevalent, control will also be easier if there are no guavas in the garden. Guavas bear over a long period and the fruit which falls to the ground is the ideal breeding habitat for the pest.

Pick of the crop

While you can grow a wide variety of fruit trees depending on your climatic region and available space, the following have been chosen because they will produce a good supply of fruit with little care or because they abundantly repay any extra care.

Brightly coloured oranges are one of the more decorative small trees.

Where a small, attractive deciduous tree is needed, heavy bearing apricots are an ideal choice.

APRICOTS

Of the many deciduous fruit trees for the home garden, the apricot is one of the most versatile. It will not only provide you with fruit which can be eaten fresh, stewed, bottled or made into jam, but also makes an attractive small shade tree with a graceful spreading habit, lovely spring blossoms and pretty autumn foliage.

Growing apricots

Apricots do best in areas with cold winters and fairly dry summers. Although they are frost resistant, they should be planted in protected positions in areas which experience late frosts to avoid any damage to the developing fruit buds. In these areas, late flowering cultivars will give the best results. Strong winds can also damage buds, flowers and developing fruit so try to protect them in areas where there are strong spring and summer winds. Allow at least 2,5-3 m between an apricot and another larger growing tree. The trees are self-pollinating and therefore do not need a pollinating partner.

Like most fruit trees, apricots will grow in a wide range of soil types, provided that the soil is well drained. In areas with poor, light soil, the holes must be very well-prepared and extra compost should be added (*see* page 19, How to plant trees).

To ensure plenty of fruit, apricot trees must be kept well watered, especially during long, dry spells. Irregular watering can result in the fruit being split. The danger periods are from spring to early summer, especially in summer rainfall regions.

Follow a routine feeding programme by fertilizing the young trees with about 750 g of 2.3.2 fertilizer in spring and then again in mid-summer. Mature trees can receive up to 1 kg per application. For healthy growth and undamaged fruit, spray regularly against fruit fly from the time the fruit reaches marble size. Using a fruit fly bait is also recommended, especially at the height of the picking season (*see* pages 25-28, Pests). Early-bearing cultivars are often less troubled by fruit fly than later types.

The trees grow vigorously and should be pruned to a vase shape or central leader shape in winter. Apricots are spur bearers so the tree must not be pruned back hard. Shorten the vigorous side shoots to 15-20 cm and leave the short shoots unpruned. Thin out the spurs if necessary. Apricot trees often send out long, tall shoots early in the growing season. Cut these back in summer to keep the height under control and to avoid heavy pruning in winter (*see* pages 33-35, Pruning).

Harvest the fruit after roughly four months. Fruit for eating or for jam-making should be picked when it is well coloured as fruit which ripens on the tree has the best flavour – do not leave it for too long as it quickly over-ripens. Fruit for bottling is best picked while still firm.

Apricots at a glance

Type of plant: Deciduous hardwood tree.
Edible parts: Fruit.
Best soil: Deep, fertile, well drained; pH 5,5-6,5.
When to plant: From container – any time; bare-rooted plants in winter.
How to plant: Into well-prepared holes.
Care: Regular watering, feeding and spraying programme.
When to harvest: When fruit is well coloured and is just soft to the touch.
How to harvest: Carefully hand-pick.
Storage: Refrigerate; bottle or make into jam.

Possible problems

Brown spots with reddish margins on the leaves, yellow speckles on leaves with rusty spots on undersides, or white deposit on leaves
Cause: Various fungal diseases
Spray with suitable fungicide.

Worms in fruit, fruit goes rotten
Cause: Fruit fly
Spray with suitable fruit fly bait.

Recommended cultivars

Alpha – large yellow freestone; vigorous grower; ripens end-November
Bulida – large light-yellow freestone with red blush; ideal for jams and preserves; ripens early December; fairly resistant to splitting
Early Cape – well-known yellow freestone, ripens mid-November
Peeka – well-flavoured orange fruit; good for eating, bottling and preserves; good garden tree; ripens late December
Piet Cellie – large yellow fruit; is subject to splitting; suited to temperate regions; heavy bearer; ripens mid-December
Royal – large yellow-orange fruit with red blush; heavy bearer; ripens late December; suited to cold winter areas

BERRIES

Not all that widely grown, boysenberries, loganberries and youngberries and the newly introduced tayberries are a rewarding addition to the food garden. While they have a relatively short fruiting season, they can produce vast quantities of fruit. Delicious to eat fresh, they can also be made into jam or used as pie fillings. The plants are all hybrids of the blackberry. Hybrid blackberries and raspberries tend to need very specialized growing conditions and so are not ideal for the home garden.

Growing berries

Boysenberries, loganberries, tayberries and youngberries grow well in most parts of the country, except those regions which experience very severe frost. Strong winds and heavy rains can cause problems to flower buds, while heavy summer rains and humid weather may spoil ripening fruit.

The berries should be planted in well-drained, fertile soil that has been enriched with generous amounts of compost. They prefer a sunny north/south-facing position, protected from strong winds and late frost.

COTTAGE CHEESE WITH BERRIES

250 g smooth cottage cheese
45 ml cream
30 ml sugar
500 g ripe youngberries, loganberries or tayberries

Beat all the ingredients together, except the berries, until smooth and creamy. Fold in the washed berries and place in fridge in one bowl or in individual bowls. Serve chilled and decorated with berries, if desired.
SERVES 4
Hint: As an alternative, use this mixture as a tasty spread on savoury biscuits.

As berries ripen quickly, they need regular picking.

Late season youngberries have large, well-shaped fruits.

Newly introduced hybrid tayberries have large, purple-black fruits.

The long, trailing canes must be supported, so the plants should be grown along a fence, preferably one which consists of strong strands of wire or a specially made trellis. To make a berry trellis, use two strong wooden or metal poles about 1,5 m high. The distance between them will depend on the space available. Attach a length of strong wire to the top of the poles, then fix a second strand about 60 cm below the first one. Plant the berries about 2,5 m apart along the trellis or fence into well-prepared planting holes.

For the best results, the berries should be kept well watered during the active growing season, especially from the time the flowers form (spring) to when the fruit is ready for harvest (mid-summer). They also need to be well fed so apply a thick layer of compost or old manure each spring and a dressing of 3.1.5 fertilizer at the rate of 70 g for young plants and up to 450 g for mature plants. Feed again in mid-summer and late summer/autumn.

Correct and routine training and pruning of the berry plants is essential for a heavy crop of fruit each season. The aim of training and pruning is to make the plant produce plenty of growth. When first planted, one or two strong canes should be allowed to grow up the trellis unpruned. In the second year, they must be trained along the top wire. Once they have finished fruiting, they must be cut down to ground level and the canes which have grown up from ground level during the summer must be tied up to take their place. Gradually allow more new canes to develop each season until you have a framework of 12-15 canes per plant, spread evenly along either side of the main stem.

The fruit should be ready for picking from mid- to late summer, depending on the type – loganberries ripen first, followed by boysenberries, tayberries and youngberries. Growing a selection will give you fruit over the longest possible period, but loganberries are slightly less prolific than the other types.

As the fruit ripens quickly, pick the berries every two to three days, first allowing the fruit to colour fully.

BERRIES AT A GLANCE

Type of plant: Trailing, deciduous cane fruit.
Edible parts: Soft berries.
Best soil: pH 6-6,5.
When to plant: Any time if in container, winter if bare-rooted.
How to plant: Into well-prepared holes.
Care: Regular watering, feed in spring, mid-summer and late summer/autumn.
When to harvest: Once fruit is well coloured and sweet.
How to harvest: Hand-pick individual berries.
Storage: Refrigerate or make into jam.

POSSIBLE PROBLEMS

Holes in developing fruit
Cause: American bollworm
Spray with herbal spray or suitable insecticide; take careful note of withholding period.

Fruit eaten
Cause: Bugs, beetles or caterpillars
Spray with herbal spray or suitable insecticide; take careful note of withholding period.

Leaves lose colour, seem to dry out
Cause: Red spider mite
Water foliage, particularly undersurfaces, during hot dry conditions with a strong jet of water; spray with suitable miticide; take careful note of withholding periods.

Grey spots develop on canes which then split
Cause: Fungal disease (anthracnose)
Always spray canes with lime sulphur just as the buds begin to swell; spray with a suitable fungicide during growing season; watering plants in the early morning helps prevent fungal diseases.

Versatile lemons deserve a place in every home garden.

CITRUS

Of all the many fruit-producing trees, citrus are among the most extensively grown, both in the home garden and commercially. Indeed, even the gardener who is not concerned with growing edible crops will want to grow at least one lemon tree. The various types of citrus trees are grown for their nutritious fruit which is especially rich in vitamin C. The fruit can be eaten fresh, squeezed for its refreshing juice or made into marmalades and preserves.

Types of citrus

While oranges and lemons are the best known types of citrus, there are many other varieties. Many new cultivars of the old favourites have been introduced, as well as some interesting and unusual hybrids. Check with your local nursery for the best ones for your area.

Growing citrus

Citrus are versatile trees which prefer mild winters and warm to hot summers. While they produce best in frost-free regions such as the Lowveld, they can be grown almost throughout the country except for areas which experience very severe frost. It is not just frost which can damage the trees – cold winds can be detrimental too. In the colder parts of the country, plant your tree in a very warm, sheltered position. Citrus also do well planted in very large containers on warm sunny patios and stoeps.

Trees, however, should also be protected from dry winds, especially in arid areas with low summer rainfall.

Citrus require good soil aeration and do best when planted in well-drained soil which is light rather than heavy. They are able to tolerate both alkaline and acid soils, but brackish conditions should be avoided.

Plant the tree in a sunny position, choosing a north-facing spot in colder regions. The planting holes must be well prepared and the trees heavily mulched after planting. Where possible, make a large, shallow well around the trees for irrigation. Allow approximately 5 m between each tree.

Regular watering during the flowering season, as well as while the fruit develops, is vital. Sudden spells with insufficient water will result in the flowers dropping and immature fruit. In summer rainfall regions, the plants must be well watered every 3-4 weeks from July/August to March. In winter rainfall regions, they will need more frequent watering – up to once a week during the long dry spells. Even while not flowering or fruiting, the trees should never be allowed to become completely dry. A heavy mulch of soil around the plant will help retain water and improve the drainage. As the trees have a shallow root system, cultivation immediately around them should be avoided.

Citrus will handsomely repay a good, regular feeding programme. Feed the trees three times a year: late winter, mid-summer and autumn. Young trees should get about 500 g of 3.1.5 fertilizer plus 50-70 g of magnesium sulphate each feed, while mature trees should receive up to 2 kg of 3.1.5 plus the same amount of magnesium.

Care should be taken when applying the fertilizer to avoid any damage to roots which are close to the surface of the soil. Before putting down the fertilizer, mulch the tree well, then spread the required amount of fertilizer in a wide circle around the tree, at least 15-20 cm away from the trunk to just under the drip line.

Citrus need little pruning and are shaped by the modified natural method (*see* Pruning, pages 33-35). All that has to be done is to remove dead twigs and branches which frequently occur inside the framework of main branches.

The Fruitful Choice

Recommended types and cultivars

Naraja – a cross between a naartjie and an orange; semi-loose-skin, firm with good flavour
Tangelo (Minneola) – a cross between a naartjie and a grapefruit; very juicy with thin skin

Limes:
Tahiti – lime with fairly large pale-yellow fruit

Naartjies:
Clementine – excellent eating naartjie with no pips
Empress – loose-skin, very juicy
Satsuma – large loose-skin with no pips
Transvaal – excellent eating with thin, firm skin

Navel oranges:
Bahianinha – thick skinned, juicy and sweet, excellent eating; ripens early from April to June
Lane Late – thin skinned, very juicy; ripens late from June to August
Palmer – sweet, juicy with thin skin, excellent eating navel

Grapefruit:
Marsh – large, light yellow, good flavour, excellent storage qualities

Dwarf citrus, such as this calamondin, make attractive container subjects.

Citrus at a glance

Type of plant: Hardwooded evergreen.
Edible parts: Fruit.
Best soil: Fertile, well drained.
When to plant: From container, any time.
How to plant: Into well-prepared individual holes.
Care: Regular watering and feeding programme.
When to harvest: When fruit has fully coloured.
How to harvest: Hand-pick.
Storage: Cool store; make into juice, marmalade or preserves.

The height of very vigorous-growing trees should be reduced by completely cutting out any tall branches to the main stem – just cutting it back will encourage more tall, rampant growth. As the trees do better if their trunks are shaded by low-hanging branches, cut the lower growth so that it is a few centimetres above the ground. A low skirt of foliage protects the trunk from the sun and helps keep the root area cool but make sure that the leaves do not touch the ground.

In most cases, the fruit can be left on the tree for many weeks and picked as required. Before picking, make sure the fruit is well coloured according to type. All limes should, however, be picked when ready and some naartjies lose quality and flavour if left to hang on the tree for too long.

Possible problems

Leaves distorted and lumpy
Cause: Citrus psylla
Spray with systemic insecticide; make careful note of withholding period.

Leaves eaten
Cause: Caterpillars
Hand-pick; spray with herbal spray or spray with suitable insecticide; note withholding period.

85

Red Blush – large, orange-red skinned fruit with red blush and pink flesh
Star Ruby – new cultivar, very juicy and sweeter than Marsh; forms a bushy, compact tree

Lemons:
Eureka – large-growing, almost thornless, with medium-large, thick-skinned juicy fruit, bears almost all year
Roughskin – large-growing, thorny tree with thick peel and yellow fruit, ripens winter
Meyer – round, smooth-skinned bitter fruit; summer fruiting

Dwarf citrus, especially good for growing in containers:
Calamondin – small, round orange-like fruits
Kumquat – very small, oblong fruits; compact growth
Chinoti – small, round oranges, compact growth

THREE FRUIT MARMALADE

2 grapefruit
2 sweet oranges
4 lemons
3 litres water
3 kg sugar

Cut all the fruit in half. Remove the pips. Take out the pith and membranes from the grapefruit. Put the pips, pith and membranes into a muslin bag.
 Cut the peel finely but cut up the flesh roughly. Put the peel, flesh and water into a pot with the bag of pips and simmer gently for 1½ hours.
 Take out the muslin bag of pips and squeeze its juice into the pot. Stir in the sugar over a low heat until it has dissolved. Boil rapidly to setting point (see below). Cool for 5 minutes, stir well, pour into hot jam jars and cover.
MAKES ABOUT 3 MEDIUM-SIZED JARS

Note: **Setting point**
Place a teaspoon of the marmalade mixture on a cold saucer and leave in a draught to cool. When cold, push the marmalade with your forefinger and if it wrinkles and a skin has formed, it is set. Test quickly to avoid overcooking.

Naartjies, with their bright colour and refreshing taste, make a welcome addition to the fruit garden.

As birds also love ripe figs, protect the fruit with netting or bird scaring devices.

FIGS

The fig is one of the oldest fruit-bearing trees known to man. While the fruit is delicious eaten raw, one of its main uses is to be made it into fig jam or special green fig 'konfyt' (preserve). As the fruit is seldom sold in shops, growing your own is often the only way to obtain it.

Growing figs

Figs are adaptable, easy-to-grow trees which crop best where the summers are warm and fairly dry and the winters cool to cold. Heavy rain in mid-summer when the fruit ripens can cause the fruit to split. The tree can be grown in almost any type of soil, but does best in deep, fertile soil with a pH of about 7. Plant it in a large, well-prepared planting hole, make a wide planting well around the soil and then mulch it thickly. As fig trees have large, vigorous root systems, they should always be planted well away from buildings and walls. Because of its wide-spreading habit, a fig tree could need as much space as 6 m but can be kept under control by regular pruning.

While the tree is able to tolerate dry conditions, it must have plenty of water during the fruiting period or the young figs will fall off. Even in summer rainfall regions, it should be watered during dry spells, while deep-soaking in winter rainfall areas and the drier parts of the country during summer is essential.

Although not greedy trees, figs respond well and give better crops if fed with 2.3.2 fertilizer in spring and mid-summer. The actual amount of fertilizer will depend on the tree, with mature trees receiving approximately 2 kg at each application.

The tree should be pruned to a vase shape or a central leader shape to encourage new side shoots. Do not open up the centre too much or the branches may suffer from sunburn. In very hot areas, the branches exposed to the sun after pruning, as well as the actual main trunk, should be painted with whitewash to stop possible sun damage.

The trees produce two crops per year under good growing conditions. The first is in early summer with the second and main crop in late summer. Figs for eating and making jam should be picked when soft to the touch, but figs for preserves must be hard.

THE FRUITFUL CHOICE

Possible problems

Pieces taken out of ripening fruit
Cause: Birds
Protect fruit with netting or tie noisy, shiny objects in the branches to scare them off.

Sawdust deposits under tree
Cause: Stem borer
Try to keep tree to one main stem; take a length of strong cloth or gauze, bury one end about 15 cm away from the trunk and then attach around the stem up to about 60 cm above the soil.

Recommended cultivars

Adam – strong grower, medium-large with brown-black skin and red flesh; ripens in January
Black Velvet – medium-large, black skin and white flesh; ripens in December
Cape Brown – small to medium, brown skin and pink flesh; ripens from January
White Genoa – medium-large, green skin and pink flesh; excellent for green fig preserve; not well suited to areas of heavy summer rain
Black Mission – purple-black with good flavour; good cultivar for summer rainfall regions

---

Figs at a glance

Type of plant: Deciduous hardwood.
Edible parts: Fruit.
Best soil: Fairly fertile; pH 7.
When to plant: From container at any time.
How to plant: Into well-prepared individual holes.
Care: Regular watering while fruit develops; fertilizer.
When to harvest: Fruit soft to touch for eating or making jam; green and hard for preserves.
How to harvest: Pick fruit from the tree.
Storage: Jam or preserves.

GRANADILLAS

Fast-growing granadillas, or passion fruit, should have a place in every home garden, provided the climate is right. These attractive fruits are invaluable in dessert making, and the pulp can also be eaten fresh or be used as a base for a delicious and refreshing fruit juice.

The granadilla originated in the tropical regions of Brazil, and while it can be grown in various areas throughout the country, it does best in warm, frost-free regions. The plant can be grown along a fence, to cover an unsightly wall or to shade a pergola or patio. Remember that granadillas are fairly short-lived plants with a productive life span of about five years, so it is a good idea to grow some young plants from seed to replace the old ones.

Growing granadillas

The plant needs a sunny position and in cooler regions make sure it is well protected from the cold by planting it in a protected north-facing aspect. It will grow in almost any soil provided that it is well drained – granadilla plants hate wet feet.

As granadillas are vigorous growers, they need plenty of space. If growing more than one plant along a wall or fence, plant the individual plants approximately 3 m apart.

Feed the plant with 200 g of 3.1.5 in spring. In warm areas where the plant should produce two crops, feed them again in late autumn. Regular feeding with a liquid feed during the active growing season will encourage plenty of new growth.

For steady growth, plenty of flowers and good fruit set, water the plant regularly, especially during long, dry spells. Keeping the plant mulched with a thick layer of compost will help retain water but still promote good drainage.

Allow the main stem of a newly planted granadilla to reach the top of its support by removing all the side stems, then pinch out the growing tip. As the new side shoots develop, tie them along the supporting wires. Because the fruit is produced on the current season's growth, you must prune the plant to encourage new shoots. After flowering, thin out weak, overcrowded or dead shoots and cut back the main stems to about 60 cm above the ground.

Possible problems

Leaves stunted or dry with white waxy substance
Cause: Mealy bug
Spray with herbal spray or suitable insecticide; note withholding period; control ants

Growth poor with hard or soft flecks on stems and leaves
Cause: Scale insects
Spray with herbal spray; use suitable insecticide; note withholding period.

GRANADILLAS AT A GLANCE

Type of plant: Evergreen vine, subtropical to warm temperate.
Edible parts: Soft pulp.
Best soil: Fertile, well drained; pH 5,5-6,5.
When to plant: Any time.
How to plant: Into well-prepared individual holes.
Care: Regular watering and feeding; keep soil mulched; spray flowers and foliage with plain water in hot, dry weather.
When to harvest: Only once fruit turns dark purple and skin begins to wrinkle.
How to harvest: Pick by hand.
Storage: Refrigerate or freeze.

Easy-to-grow granadillas make useful climbers up fences or against walls.

GRAPES

Nothing can quite equal the pleasure of being able to pick your own home-grown bunches of delicious, juicy grapes. While the plants themselves grow very easily, the fruit does need some extra care for the best results.

Grapevines in the home garden serve a double purpose – apart from their fruit, the plants make an ideal covering for a pergola over a 'stoep' or patio, or they can be trained to cover arbours and walkways, and can also make a useful garden screen. Being deciduous, they provide plenty of shade over outdoor living areas during the hot summer months, but allow in welcome light and sunshine during winter.

In most areas during autumn, especially those with cold, dry conditions, the leaves turn glorious shades of yellow and red before they fall.

Success with growing grapes depends to a large degree on choosing the right type of grapes for your area. There are a number of new cultivars available, bred especially for the Highveld and summer rainfall regions.

GROWING GRAPES

Grapes need plenty of sunshine in order for the bunches to ripen properly. They also need good air circulation to lessen the risk of fungal diseases, so always choose a warm, sunny, fairly open spot, preferably one which gets full morning sun when planting grapes.

For heavy, healthy crops year after year, always follow a regular watering, feeding, pruning and spraying routine. When vines are grown up a pergola or a high trellis, early training to achieve a good framework of fruit-bearing wood is also vital.

During the active growing season when the vines are producing their flowers and setting their fruit, they must be kept well watered. As the bunches of grapes reach maturity, the plants should receive less water but should never be allowed to dry out so that the leaves begin to wilt.

A wide variety of grapes can be grown – but choose cultivars best suited to your local conditions.

Food from your Garden

1. Tie the young vine to its support – the plant must be cut back to a strong growing point.

2. Allow the young vine to grow to the top of the pergola. Tie the vine to the pergola – cut off any shoots which develop up the support to encourage it to grow in length.

3. In the second and third winters, thin out the side shoots to about 20-50 cm apart and tie to the cross supports.

4. In subsequent winters, cut back the shoots to about three buds. Train the shoots over the pergola to form a strong framework.

Grapes at a Glance

Type of plant: Deciduous, hardwooded, fruit-bearing, perennial climber or shrub.
Edible parts: Harvested bunches of berries.
Best soil: Fertile, well-drained loam; pH 5,5-6,5.
When to plant: From a container, at any time of year – most suitable planting times winter and early spring, depending on climate.
How to plant: In large, well-prepared individual holes.
Care: Regular feeding and watering with careful attention to preventative control of insect pests and diseases.
When to harvest: Only once bunches are fully ripened.
How to harvest: Cut bunches off vine with a sharp, long, pointed pair of scissors.
Storage: Refrigerate.

Remember, however, that grapes do not ripen after they have been picked. The bunches must be left on the vine until they have fully developed their true flavour and colour. Once all the bunches have been picked, water the plants well. They now have a second growth period which helps them to develop growth before the winter and encourages new root development.

Feed established vines with 2.3.2 fertilizer in spring at the rate of between 750 g and 2,5 kg, depending on their age. Give much older vines up to 5 kg of 2.3.2 but this should be divided into two applications to prevent any possible root damage. In mid-summer, apply a dressing of LAN fertilizer at the rate of

250 g to 1 kg, depending on age. As vines can suffer from a magnesium deficiency, give the plants a dressing of 500 g Epsom salts each spring. Vines also like a slightly acid soil with a pH of between 5,5 and 6,5. If you are uncertain of the pH levels of the soil where the grapes are growing, have it tested or test it yourself.

To help prevent fungal diseases which can often become serious problems, vines must be sprayed after pruning with lime sulphur. Once the vines come into growth, begin to flower and set fruit, they should get regular protection from fungal diseases and insect pests.

POSSIBLE PROBLEMS

White or grey powdery deposits on shoots, flowers, fruit and leaves
Cause: Powdery mildew
Always spray in winter with lime sulphur and during early growth period with suitable fungicide.

Ripening fruit goes soft and rotten with mouldy appearance
Cause: Grey mould
Spray with suitable fungicide three weeks before harvest and again one week before if conditions are wet.

Leaves develop oily looking patches, turn yellow and dry out; white or brown deposits on undersides of the leaves; white powder on fruit
Cause: Downy mildew
Spray with a suitable fungicde when the shoots are about 20 cm long. In areas where this is a serious problem, such as the south western Cape, spray regularly every fortnight during the growing season.
Note: Spraying in winter with lime sulphur helps control a number of other pests as well.

Fruit does not form properly; bunches become malformed and are very small
Cause: Various insect pests such as snout beetle, bollworm and fruit beetle
Hand-pick where possible or spray with a herbal spray. Use a suitable chemical pesticide, but take careful note of safety periods.

Leaves severely damaged with large holes or completely eaten
Cause: Various insect pests such as chafer beetles and hawk moth caterpillar
Hand-pick where possible or spray with a herbal spray. Use a suitable chemical pesticide, but take careful note of the safety periods.

Holes in individual berries which then go rotten
Cause: Various birds, especially sparrows, starlings and mouse birds
Cover whole vine with light plastic or cloth net if possible or put net bags or brown paper bags over the ripening bunches. Noisy, glittering objects hung in the vine, for example strips of aluminium foil, also help deter birds.

RECOMMENDED CULTIVARS

Table grapes suitable for growing in the home garden:

In order of ripening
Highveld and summer rainfall regions
Pirobella – Small reddish-black grape; ripens mid-December; reliable cultivar with well-formed bunches; well suited to Highveld and summer rainfall regions
Bien Donne – Medium-white grape with slight nutmeg flavour; ripens from end-December to February; resistant to berry crack; well suited to Highveld conditions
Earlihane – Medium-white grape; ripens end December; vigorous grower with strong Hanepoot flavour; well suited to summer rainfall regions
Ronelle – Large, dark red, round grape; ripens in January; bred for Highveld conditions
Dan-ben-Hannah – Large, oval red-black grape; ripens mid-January; vigorous grower; heavy bearer; resistant to berry crack; suited to all areas

Winter rainfall regions
Queen of the Vineyard – Large, oval white grape; ripens end December
Dan-ben-Hannah – Large, oval red-black grape; ripens mid-January; vigorous grower and heavy bearer; resistant to berry crack
Alphonse Lavalle – Large black grape; ripens mid-February; popular grape with excellent flavour
Waltham Cross – Large, oval white to light amber grape; ripens in February; tough skinned with few seeds
Hanepoot – Large, round red or white fruited grape; ripens February to March; soft skinned, very sweet; fruit can be prone to fungal diseases

---

GREEN GRAPE MOULD

500 g unripe grapes
1 litre water
sugar to taste
pinch of bicarbonate of soda
pinch of salt
250 ml sago
2 eggs, separated
strawberries for garnish

Boil all the ingredients together, except the sago, eggs and strawberries, until the grapes are soft. Do not drain. Rub the grapes through a sieve and return pulp to saucepan. Add the sago and simmer until the sago has thickened and cooked. Sweeten to taste and allow to cool.

Beat egg yolks and add to mixture. Beat whites until stiff and fold into mixture. Pour into a glass bowl or jelly mould and chill. Turn out and garnish with strawberries. Serve with cold custard or ice cream.
SERVES 4-6

Food from your Garden

Rich in vitamin C, guavas are easy to grow and make attractive garden trees.

GUAVAS

Guavas are among the most popular of all fruits, mainly because of their exceptionally high vitamin C content. The fruit can be eaten raw or cooked, it can be bottled, made into jam or jelly, or even be made into fruit juice. Quick-growing, prolific producers, they are worth the little extra care needed for unspoilt fruit.

Growing guavas

Originating from the tropics, guavas are nonetheless very adaptable. They thrive in the warmer areas, but do well in cooler regions provided they are sheltered from frost and cold winds. They will also grow in virtually any soil as long as it is well drained. A guava tree should be planted in a sunny position about 5 m from another guava or other tree. The tree must be kept well watered, especially during dry spells when it is flowering and while the fruit is setting. Sudden dry conditions will lead to flower and fruit drop. For the best results, feed in early summer and again in autumn. Use about 250 g of 3.1.5 each feed for young trees and up to 2 kg each feed for older trees.

The tree should be pruned in October. It needs hard pruning into a vase shape and tall branches should be cut back to reduce height and encourage plenty of fruiting side shoots.

The fruit is ready to pick when it is soft to the touch and the skin has turned from green to yellow.

As fruit fly can be a serious problem in the home garden, a regular spray programme may be needed to control these pests in some areas.

Possible problems

Fruit has worms and goes rotten
Cause: Fruit fly
Spray with suitable insecticide early in the season only, then use a fruit fly bait; splash bait on leaves every week and again after heavy rain.

Recommended cultivars

Fan Retief – large, pink fleshed, all-purpose grape.
Adam – medium brown with dark red flesh; strong-growing, all-purpose fruit
Cape Brown – small to medium with pink flesh

Guavas at a glance

Type of plant: Evergreen hardwood.
Edible parts: Fruit.
Best soil: Well drained; pH 6-6,5.
When to plant: From a container, any time.
How to plant: Well-prepared individual holes.
Care: Regular watering during flowering and fruit set.
When to harvest: When fruit is just soft to the touch and well coloured.
How to harvest: Hand-pick.
Storage: Jam or jelly; bottle or make into juice.

Typically large, round-fruited pawpaws give a distinct tropical feel to a garden.

PAWPAWS

Sweet, juicy and nutritious, pawpaws make the ideal breakfast fruit and are an important ingredient in a fruit salad. They can also be made into pickles, jams and preserves and are sometimes even cooked like marrow. With their unusual growth habit, they make interesting and decorative garden plants.

GROWING PAWPAWS

Although tropical in origin, pawpaw trees are fairly adaptable. They naturally thrive in the subtropical parts of the country such as the Lowveld and the Natal coast, but can be grown in cooler parts too. They will also survive in light frost areas provided they are planted in a very warm, protected spot. In most gardens, the best position is one which is warm and sunny and protected from the wind and cold. They do especially well in cooler regions when planted near walls or in sheltered corners or courtyards but need air circulation in hot, humid environments. The plants will grow in most soils but must have good drainage. They respond well to compost but manures are best avoided.

Unlike practically all other types of commonly grown fruit, pawpaws are dioecious which means that the male and female flowers are produced on separate plants. It is sometimes possible to get bisexual plants which are self-pollinating. Their fruits, which have a good flavour, are long and narrow rather than the typically large, round-fruited pawpaws but the plants need much warmer conditions then the others. Small-fruited pawpaws, known as papino or Solo pawpaws, are being increasingly grown commercially.

Pawpaw trees are grown from seed although you can root soft heel cuttings. Remember to take seed only from a ripe pawpaw which has an exceptionally good flavour. The seed should be washed and dried and then stored in an airtight container until planting time which is mid- to late summer. Sow a couple of groups of five seeds, each with about 1-2 m between the groups, into well-prepared soil. You can also raise your seed in deep seed trays or small pots and then transplant them when they are about 20 cm tall.

As it is impossible to tell the male seedlings from the female ones, you have to wait until the plants flower to select the males and females. Do not discard thin, weak seedlings before they flower as these are often the females. The plants will start to flower once they are about a metre high. The female flowers are larger than the male flowers and are produced singly or in a small cluster and have short flower stalks. The male flowers appear in long, branched, hanging clusters which can be up to a metre long under ideal conditions. When pawpaws are sold in nurseries, 3-4 seedlings are sold in one container.

One male pawpaw plant will be able to pollinate up to 20 female ones, so keep one strong male in the garden and as many females as you have space for.

Feed the plants from spring to late summer with about 100 g of 2.3.2 per plant. Mulch well before applying fertilizer but do not let the mulch touch the stem as it could cause root rot. Be very careful not to damage the stem in any way and keep cultivation round the plants to a minimum. Keep the plants well watered during the active growing and fruiting season, especially during long dry spells.

The fruit is ready to pick once it has turned yellow but if fruiting pests such as bats are a problem, pick while the fruit is still slightly green – pawpaws ripen well after harvesting.

The plants produce their best crops over the first two to three fruiting seasons, after which the quality and quantity of the pawpaw declines. In the home garden it is therefore better to discard the older plants and to rather replace them with new ones.

Possible problems

White powdery deposit on young leaves, leaves turn brown, fruit also affected
Cause: Powdery mildew
Dust regularly with sulphur or use a wettable sulphur spray; try only growing strains which are known to be resistant.

Young growth distorted and curly
Cause: Aphids
Spray with strong jet of water; use a herbal spray or spray with a suitable insecticide, take careful note of withholding period.

Pawpaws at a glance

Type of plant: Softwooded perennial; subtropical.
Edible parts: Fruit.
Best soil: Fertile; very well drained; pH 6-6,5.
When to plant: From seed in summer; established young plants from container any time.
How to plant: Seedlings sown into well-prepared soil.
Care: Plenty of water in summer, less in winter; fertilize in spring to late summer.
When to harvest: When fruit turns yellow or when it is still slightly green.
How to harvest: Carefully pick by hand.
Storage: Refrigerate.

Small-fruited papino pawpaws are becoming increasingly popular for their delicious taste.

Pawpaw as a tenderizer

If you are worried about meat being tough, add a few pawpaw seeds to about 125 ml pawpaw juice and pour over the meat to tenderize it before cooking. Alternatively, wrap the meat in some lightly bruised pawpaw leaves and leave in the fridge for a couple of hours.

Brandied peaches

3 kg small, ripe peaches
2 kg sugar
1,5 litres water
brandy

Dip the peaches in hot water one at a time and rub off the fur with a soft cloth. Put the sugar and water into a pot and dissolve the sugar slowly over a low heat. Bring to the boil and allow to boil for 10 minutes without any stirring.

Carefully add the peaches to the syrup, a couple at a time, and simmer for about 5 minutes until tender. Gently lift out the peaches with a slotted spoon and pack into hot preserving jars.

Leave the syrup to simmer until thick. Allow to cool and then measure out the syrup. Boil the syrup with an equal quantity of brandy. Pour into jars and fill to the top. Seal the jars tightly and store in a cool place. The longer you leave them the better!
MAKES ABOUT 3 MEDIUM-SIZED JARS

PEACHES AND NECTARINES

Nothing really beats the flavour of sun-ripened peaches. Best eaten fresh, these delicious fruits can also be made into jams or bottled. While they may look very different, nectarines are essentially smooth-skinned peaches and are grown in exactly the same way.

GROWING PEACHES AND NECTARINES

As with most of the deciduous fruit, the right climate and choice of cultivar is important. The trees fruit best where the winters are cool to cold and the summers warm. If the winter temperatures do not drop sufficiently, the tree may not be properly dormant in winter and may suffer from premature bud drop. In areas subject to late frost, late flowering types should be chosen.

Peaches and nectarines are self-pollinating so only one tree is needed for a good crop. Where space permits and conditions are favourable, early, mid- and late season cultivars can be grown. The trees, however, do need space and good air circulation and must be planted 3-5 m away from each other or any other large trees.

The trees need the same feeding and care programme as apricots do. Peaches and nectarines can be pruned into a vase shape or by the central leader method. They produce fruit on the new wood from the previous growing season. Basic pruning should entail shortening back long branches by about a third and removing crisscrossing shoots.

As yellow clingstone trees bear more fruit from the tips of the new growth, they must be more lightly pruned back. Before pruning all types, check to see where the fruit buds are situated and then cut back so that a good number remain (*see* pages 33-35, Pruning).

Most peach and nectarine cultivars bear heavy crops and the fruit should be thinned so that you get individual fruit of a good size. Thinning the fruit also encourages the development of new side shoots. Begin thinning the fruit early in the season when the immature fruit is about the size of a small marble, then thin out again when it is about the size of a small egg, leaving approximately 10 cm between each fruit.

Peaches and nectarines must be picked and handled extremely carefully as they bruise easily. The fruit which is allowed to ripen on the tree until it is just soft to the touch has the best flavour but you may have to pick it slightly under-ripe if fruit fly and other pests are a serious problem. However, the fruit still ripens well after it has been picked provided it is well developed. Place unripened fruit in flat trays so that it does not touch.

The little extra care needed for fresh, blemish-free fruit is well worthwhile when lovely peaches like these are produced.

Possible problems

Fruit has worms and goes rotten
Cause: Fruit fly, codling moth or false codling moth
Spray every 14 days from the time the fruit is marble sized.

Leaves are distorted with lumpy pink blisters
Cause: Peach leaf curl
Spray with suitable fungicide, i.e. lime sulphur in winter and with a copper-based spray as the buds begin to swell.

Recommended cultivars

In order of ripening:
Peaches
De Wet – green-yellow freestone dessert peach with yellow flesh; ripens early to mid-October
Desert Gold – large, yellow-red, yellow-fleshed dessert, semi-clingstone peach; ripens mid-October
Orion – large freestone peach with red blush and white flesh; resistant to delayed foliation; ripens end-October
Earlibelle – creamy white peach with red blush and white flesh; ripens mid-November; needs cold winter
Sunray – medium-sized, orange-yellow peach with yellow flesh; good for eating and bottling; ripens mid-November
Early Dawn – creamy-yellow with red blush and yellow flesh; ripens mid-November; needs cold winter
Culemborg – large yellow-red blush, greenish-white flesh, semi-clingstone dessert peach; heavy bearer; ripens mid-November; fairly resistant to delayed foliation

---

Peaches and nectarines at a glance

Type of plant: Deciduous hardwood; temperate to cold climate.
Edible parts: Fruit.
Best soil: Fertile, well drained; pH 5,5-6,5.
When to plant: From a container, any time; bare-rooted in winter.
How to plant: Into well-prepared holes.
Care: Routine feeding, watering and spraying programme.
When to harvest: Once fruit is just soft to the touch.
How to harvest: Carefully pick by hand.
Storage methods: Make into jam

Rhodes/Swellengrebel – greeny-white peach with red blush and white flesh; excellent flavour; ripens late November
Van Riebeeck – green-white peach with red blush and white flesh, freestone; keeps well; ripens mid-December; fairly resistant to delayed foliation
Safari – large, orange-yellow skinned and orange-fleshed heavy bearing peach, ripens mid-December; moderately resistant to delayed foliation
Oom Sarel – excellent eating and bottling peach with yellow skin and yellow flesh; ripens in mid- to late December; resistant to delayed foliation
Professor Malherbe – *see* Oom Sarel
Kakamas – golden-yellow clingstone peach with yellow flesh; resistant to delayed foliation; good bottling peach
Elberta – well-known large, yellow-green freestone peach with red blush and yellow flesh; ripens in January; needs cold winter

Nectarines
Armking – large, dark-red nectarine with yellow flesh; ripens from mid-November onwards
Sunlite – large, yellow clingstone nectarine with red blush, ripens mid-November onwards
Goldmine – green-white skinned nectarine with dark red blush and white flesh; strong grower and heavy bearer; ripens mid-January

To give the fruit space to develop, thin out excess fruitlets when they are still small.

THE FRUITFUL CHOICE

Juicy and full of flavour, plums are amongst the easiest of deciduous fruit trees to grow.

PLUMS

For ease of cultivation, minimal care and lack of insect pests, plums are the top choice among the various deciduous fruit trees to grow in your garden. They also make attractive small shade trees with lovely spring blossom and should have a place in every food-producing garden provided the climate is right. The fruit is eaten raw, stewed, or made into jams and preserves.

GROWING PLUMS

Like peaches and nectarines, some cultivars do better in areas with cold winters because of delayed foliation. However, there are also a number of cultivars which are very adaptable and can be grown in most parts of the country, with the exception of the very hot and humid areas. As some cultivars need pollinating partners if they are to produce heavy crops, concentrate on planting the self-fertile cultivars, particularly if you have space for only one or two trees. Choosing cultivars which fruit at different times will give you fruit over a much longer season.

Plums grow easily in most soils, but prefer a well-drained, fairly deep soil with a pH range of between 5,5 and 7. Plant the trees into well-prepared planting holes in a fairly wind-sheltered position, especially in areas of strong spring and summer winds.

Depending on the cultivar, plums should be planted about 3-5 m apart from each other or away from other large trees. Although not excessively demanding, they will respond well to regular watering, especially during long, dry spells. For example, the trees should be watered every 3 weeks in the winter in the summer rainfall regions, and every 2-3 weeks during summer in winter rainfall regions. The trees should also be kept watered about once a week during the critical flowering and bud setting period. For really abundant crops every season, follow the fertilizing programme for apricots (*see* page 81). Like peaches, plums are heavy bearers and larger, better quality fruit will result if the fruit is thinned when still tiny, about the size of a small marble, and then again when it is about the size of a small egg. This second thinning is not essential but will result in bigger fruit. The trees can be pruned either to a vase shape or by the central leader method.

Probably the biggest advantage that plums have over their other deciduous relations is that they are far less susceptible to pest damage, especially fruit fly. They therefore do not need a vigorous spray routine – a winter spray of lime sulphur is all that is usually necessary. One problem which can occur is pear slug but even this can be quickly controlled (*see* page 27).

PLUMS AT A GLANCE

Type of plant: Deciduous hardwood; temperate to cold climate.
Edible parts: Fruit.
Best soil: Fertile, well drained; pH 5,5-7.
When to plant: From a container, any time; bare-rooted in winter.
How to plant: Into well-prepared holes.
Care: Routine feeding, watering and spraying programme.
When to harvest: Once fruit is just soft to the touch.
How to harvest: Carefully pick

POSSIBLE PROBLEMS

Fruit has worm and goes rotten
Cause: Fruit fly (not common)
Spray every 14 days from time fruit is about marble-sized.

Leaves eaten away with just the skeleton left
Cause: Pear slug
Spray with herbal spray or use a suitable insecticide.

FOOD FROM YOUR GARDEN

RECOMMENDED CULTIVARS

Methley – small red plums with red flesh; very heavy bearer; self-pollinating; resistant to delayed foliation; ideal for the home garden; ripens from late November to January, depending on the region
Santa Rosa – large, juicy, top quality dark red plums with dark red flesh; heavy and reliable bearers; produces better crops when pollinated by Satsuma or Wickson; ripens December; fairly susceptible to delayed foliation
Wickson – large, heart-shaped, green-yellow plum with a red blush; upright growth habit; cross-pollinate with Santa Rosa; ripens late December/January; fairly susceptible to delayed foliation
Harry Pickstone – medium-sized, dark red fruit with sweet, juicy yellow flesh; excellent for home garden; self-pollinating and resistant to delayed foliation; ripens mid-January
Satsuma – dark red, large-sized plums with purple-red flesh; good, reliable bearer; cross-pollinate with Wickson or Santa Rosa; ripens from about January to February; fairly reistant to delayed foliation

If you have limited space, always choose self-pollinating plum cultivars, such as Harry Pickstone.

PLUM AND APPLE JAM

1 kg plums
1 kg apples
750 ml water
1,5 kg sugar

Wash the plums, cut them in half and remove the stones. Peel and core apples and cut into slices. Put the prepared fruit and water into a heavy-based pot and simmer until soft. Stir in the sugar over a low heat until dissolved. Boil briskly until setting point (see Note on page 86) is reached, then pour into hot jam jars and cover. Store in a cool place.
MAKES ABOUT 4 MEDIUM-SIZED JARS

Bright red, freshly picked strawberries make a wonderful sweet dessert.

STRAWBERRIES

To the majority of home gardeners, fruit is something you pick off a tree or a vine. One exception to this rule is the delectable strawberry. This popular fruit is usually served fresh as a dessert with cream and sugar, or is often made into jam. It has a high vitamin C content, is sweet-scented and delicious to taste. A flat, trailing perennial, it needs very different care to most fruits but is extremely rewarding and can provide large quantities of sweet, succulent fruit in a very small area.

GROWING STRAWBERRIES

Strawberries grow in a wide range of climatic conditions. As some types do better in specific areas, only grow those recommended by local growers. The plants like a well-drained, sandy-loam

Black plastic sheeting helps keep the fruit clean and retain moisture.

soil which has been thoroughly prepared with well-rotted organic matter. They also prefer an acid soil of between 5,5 and 6,5 so alkaline soils may need to be adjusted to suit them (*see* pages 13-15).

In the home garden, strawberries are best planted in separate beds but can be used as an edging to vegetable beds. You can also grow strawberries in containers such as a strawberry barrel (*see* page 37).

To prepare the soil for strawberries, spread a thick layer – up to 15 cm – of well-rotted manure and compost over the soil, and a dressing of 250 g of 2.3.2 fertilizer per m². To poor soils, add a little bone meal as well. Dig the soil over to a depth of about 25 cm and work the soil until it has a fine, crumbly texture, then rake it level and water thoroughly. If possible, prepare the beds 2-3 weeks in advance to give the soil time to settle.

Young strawberry plants are usually set out from late summer to autumn. The plants should be planted about 30 cm apart with 30 cm between the rows. Make sure that the crown of the plant – where the roots and leaves join – is just on ground level. They must get ample water if they are to flower and fruit well. Water 2-3 times a week while flowering and setting fruit; reduce the amount of water as the fruits start to ripen but never allow plants to dry out.

Mulching the plants with straw, wood, wool or plastic sheeting helps to retain vital soil moisture and helps keep the fruit clean. Black plastic sheeting has the advantage of also protecting the plants from slugs, snails and other insect pests. Provided the soil has been very well prepared, the plastic sheeting can be laid over the bed and the plants planted in holes made in the plastic.

As the plants begin to flower, feed them with 3.1.5 fertilizer at the rate of 60 g per m². Once the fruit has set, feed them with a balanced liquid fertilizer high in potassium. Plants grown in plastic sheeting can only be fed with liquid fertilizer.

Strawberries have the best flavour if they are allowed to ripen completely on the plant. Wait until they are deep red and protect them from bird damage by covering them with netting.

Strawberries will produce a number of runners per plant. If left on, the quantity and quality of the fruit from the parent plant diminishes. Allow one or two runners to develop and use these as replacement plants.

Strawberries produce good yields for about 3-4 years and then must be replaced with new plants. Only use your own plants if your stock is disease free and produces good quality fruit.

Possible problems

Fruit eaten
Cause A: Birds
Protect plants by covering with netting or make a special wire netting frame or tie shiny strips of aluminium foil onto the top branches.

Cause B: Slugs and snails
Mulch with plastic sheeting; put down snail bait or use non-toxic methods.

Fruit goes rotten, with grey fungus
Cause: Botrytis
Aggravated by moist, humid conditions and over-feeding with nitrogen; water plants carefully in the early morning; mulch with plastic sheeting; spray with a suitable fungicide; burn infected fruit and foliage.

Recommended cultivars

As strawberries are extremely prone to incurable viral diseases, be sure that you only plant Government certified virus-free stock, which is normally available from reputable nurseries and garden centres. Old varieties which have been growing in gardens for a number of years are almost sure to be infected.

Parfaite – large fruit, strong grower; does well in winter rainfall regions
Rolinda – similar to Parfaite, but with better flavour and firmer fruit
Selekta – large, firm fruit; good flavour; vigorous, heavy bearer; winter bearing in frost-free regions
Tiobelle – medium-sized firm fruit; bright red; heavy bearer

Strawberries at a glance

Type of plant: Berry-producing, clump-forming perennial.
Edible parts: Berries.
Best soil: Fertile, well drained; pH 5,5-6,5.
When to plant: Autumn.
How to plant: 30 cm apart; rows 30 cm apart.
Care: Water regularly, protect from pests.
When to harvest: When fruit is fully ripe.
How to harvest: Hand-pick.
Storage: Refrigerate; make jam.

FOOD FROM YOUR GARDEN

OTHER FRUIT AND NUT TREES IN BRIEF

ALMONDS

An attractive small tree with pretty blossom, it produces the best crops in areas with warm, dry summers and no late frosts. The tree needs plenty of water during the active growing season but heavy rain in summer can spoil the nuts. The tree should be protected from strong prevailing summer winds. All almonds need cross-pollination.
Recommended cultivars: Britz, IXL, Papershell and Non Pareil

APPLES

Apples are not well suited to the warm to hot parts of the country and most of the Highveld. They do best in cool to cold winter regions and are grown commercially in the southern and western Cape, but some varieties will fruit in warmer regions. The trees must be cross-pollinated for successful crops so a minimum of two trees must be grown. A strict spraying programme is needed against fruit fly and codling moth and the tree must be well fed and watered. Apples are pruned to a vase shape or by the central leader method.
Recommended cultivars: Alma, Golden Delicious, Granny Smith, Starking

Almonds and macadamias are heavy bearers.

Good results can be obtained from home-grown bananas in the hot, humid parts of the country.

AVOCADO

Medium to large-growing trees, usually with wide-spreading habit, the avocado makes a good garden specimen. It prefers warm, frost-free regions, but can be grown in cooler areas if well sheltered. Keep trees well watered, especially during long, dry spells in summer; mulching the soil will help retain moisture. Feed in late winter, mid-summer and autumn with 3.1.5 fertilizer. Avocados grown from pips seldom bear good fruit and will take more than seven years to flower.
Recommended cultivars: Edranol, Fuerte and Hass

BANANAS

Bananas can only be grown successfully in the hot, humid parts of the country, especially well suited to the Natal coast. They need plenty of moisture at all times and regular feeding.
Recommended cultivars: Dwarf Cavendish and Williams

KIWI FRUITS

An increasingly popular commercial fruit, this fruiting vine has rather specific growing conditions. It does best in cool climates with moderate rainfall; late spring frost can damage flower buds. Like pawpaws, kiwis are dioecious and one male is usually sufficient to pollinate about five females. The plants like plenty of water, espcially in dry spells during summer.

LITCHIS

These are very large-growing trees suitable for subtropical regions only. They need plenty of moisture, good soil and regular feeding.

MACADAMIAS

Macadamias are large-growing trees which bear small, hard-shelled, protein-rich nuts. They are best suited to temperate regions with good summer rainfall. Only plant grafted macadamia trees, not seedlings.

MANGOES

Extremely large-growing trees, mangoes are only suited to subtropical regions; they need to be kept dry in winter and bud very well. Water trees once flowers form. Feed in winter, early summer, mid-summer and autumn and only plant grafted trees.
Recommended cultivars: Heidi, Peach, Sensation and Kent

Pears

Pear trees are not well suited to warmer regions and prefer cool to cold winters and mild summers. The trees must be cross-pollinated and need a strict spraying and feeding programme. Prune to the vase or central leader method.
Recommended cultivars: Packham's Triumph, Bon Chretien, Beurre Bosc and Keiffer

Pecan nuts

Successful only in the subtropics, pecan nut trees need a long growing season with warm days and nights and mild winters. Very large trees, they are not well suited to the home garden.
Recommended cultivars: Barton, Desirable and Wichita

Quinces

A particularly easy-to-grow tree, it grows well in all regions except the subtropics. Treat them like apples and pears although quinces do not need as much fertilizer for good crops. The fruit is ideal for jam, jelly and bottling.
Recommended variety: Cape Selected

Grow Cape gooseberries during summer.

Edible and decorative, interesting and unusual fruits

There are a number of shrubs and trees which, although they produce delicious fruits, are not widely grown for this purpose. These include cherry guavas, pineapple guavas and persimmons, while tree tomatoes and Cape gooseberries make a welcome addition to the family's menu.

Cape gooseberries

A shrubby perennial plant, the Cape gooseberry is a relative of the tomato and likes similar warm growing conditions. While established plants can be bought, Cape gooseberries are easy to grow from seed. They do best in rich soil and should be kept well fed and watered during the growing season and sprayed against red spider mite.

Cherry guavas

An attractive, easy-to-grow relative of the large fruiting guava, it produces masses of small red fruits with a pleasant, rather strawberry-like flavour. While the fruit can be made into jam, it is at its best when picked and eaten straight from the tree.

Persimmons

An attractive deciduous small tree which grows best in warm, temperate to subtropical regions, the tree must be kept well watered and fed. The secret with persimmons is to allow the fruit to ripen fully as the unripe fruit has an unpleasantly tart flavour. Normally two trees are needed for successful cross-pollination. Tree-ripened fruit has the best flavour but fully formed, well-coloured, firm fruit will ripen indoors.
Recommended cultivars: Diospuros, Kaki, Fuju, Mezerelli and Tipu

Pineapple guavas

Pineapple guavas prefer warm, temperate conditions. They produce waxy green fruits 5-7 cm long. Their flavour is a combination of granadilla, guava and pineapple, but they sare only ready to eat when fully mature. They should be allowed to drop off the trees on their own, rather than be picked, then kept to ripen indoors for another week or so until the fruit is soft and develops its characteristic fruity aroma.

Tree tomatoes are attractive garden specimens.

Tree tomatoes

Widely grown in New Zealand, the tree tomato can be grown in many frost-free regions and even in cooler parts if in a well-protected spot. Also called tamarillo, it makes an interesting small shrub which produces fragrant, pale pink flowers followed by clusters of egg-shaped fruits. These turn orange-red when ripe and taste like a slightly sweet tomato. If eaten raw, the skin must be removed as it has an unpleasant taste. The fruit can be added to fruit salad or stewed, bottled or made into jam.

Herbs are easy to grow and have a myriad medicinal and culinary uses.

HERBS

The term 'herb' covers a wide range of seed-bearing plants, from low-growing ground covers like pennyroyal to woody shrubs and trees such as lavender, rosemary and bay leaf. The various herbs also have a number of different uses, with the culinary use of herbs being probably the most important as far as the home gardener is concerned.

The majority of herbs are extremely easy to grow and, with a few exceptions, prefer a sunny position and well-drained soil. While they will grow with very little attention, they naturally do that much better if they are fed and watered regularly. Being so versatile, herbs can be grown in a number of places. Planting a selection of herbs in a special herb garden is a popular method that has a long tradition, but herbs can just as easily be grown in beds and borders, containers, troughs and window boxes.

As well as their culinary, medicinal and cosmetic uses, however, a number of herbs make excellent companion plants to vegetables and fruit trees and should therefore be an integral part of any food garden.

The smaller types, such as parsley, garlic, chives, mint and thyme, can be used to edge vegetable and flower beds, while taller ones such as tarragon and chervil can be given their own place in the vegetable garden or can even be grown between rows of vegetables, as well as in beds and borders and near fruit trees. Herbs, with their aromatic fragrance, are a must in any garden.

Lavender and parsley help ward off pests and diseases on these lettuces.

What is companion planting?

Before the advent of synthetic fertilizers and pesticides, gardeners and farmers alike had to rely on natural growing methods to produce healthy plants. From experience gleaned over hundreds of years, they knew that certain plants grew better when planted alongside other types and that a wide range of plants, especially the common herbs, had insect repellent properties, either through their leaves or roots, while others such as legumes improved the fertility of the soil. As well as good companions, however, there were also plants which did not grow well together.

The art of growing particular plants together, known as companion planting, has tended to be superseded by chemical products because these are easy to use and have quick-acting, easily visible results. However, the increasing awareness of the dangers to the environment through pollution of the atmosphere, soil and water sources, as well as the possible dangers to health from residues left in or on fruit and vegetables, has made more and more people prefer to use natural growing methods and environmentally friendly products.

On their own, companion plants are unlikely to totally control pests and diseases or make any marked difference to the soil, but they do become a vital tool in gardening when they are used as part of an organic gardening programme (*see* pages 17-18).

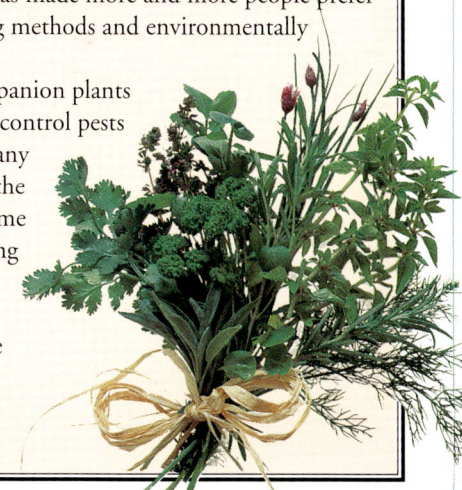

Plants and their Good Companions

PLANT	COMPANION	WHAT IS ACHIEVED
Apple	Chives	Less chance of apple scab disease
	Wormwood and garlic	Protection from codling moth
Beans	Marigold	Repels beetles
	Petunia	Beans less likely to suffer from beetles
	Summer savory	Beans grow more strongly
Beetroot	Onions	Beetroot grows better
Broccoli	Dill or mint	Broccoli grows better
Cabbage	Rosemary or sage	Repels cabbage butterfly
	Celery	Helps control grubs on cabbage
Carrots	Dill	Chemical secreted by dill improves health of carrots
	Sage or onions	Carrot fly is repelled
Celery	Bush beans	Help each other grow better
Eggplant	*Amaranthus* or nasturtium	Less likelihood of insects on eggplants
	Beans	Beetles repelled from eggplant
Fruit trees	Garlic	In a circle at base of tree it deters borers
Grapes	Clover or lupins	Increases soil fertility
	Hyssop	Vine crop increases
Leeks	Celery or onions	Leeks grow better
Lettuce	Chervil	Protection from aphids, snails and mildew
Peach	Garlic	Reduces chance of peach leaf curl
Potatoes	Beans	Potatoes less likely to suffer from beetle damage
Radish	Beans	Both grow better
	Lettuce	In summer, radish more tasty
Sweetcorn	Sunflower	Provides increased nitrogen to corn
Strawberries	Borage	Soil nutrition improves for strawberries
	Marigold	Helps control nematodes
Tomatoes	Marigold	Tomatoes grow and produce better
	Basil	Improves flavour and growth
	Thyme or peppermint	Helps control white fly

Attractive, aromatic and insect repelling herbs play a vital role in the food-producing garden.

FOOD FROM YOUR GARDEN

BAD COMPANIONS

The following plants are said to have bad effects on each other:

◆ Beans with beetroot, onions, fennel or chives;
◆ Cabbage with grapes, onions, rue or tomatoes;
◆ Carrot with anise, dill or wormwood;
◆ Fennel with coriander, beans or peppers;
◆ Potatoes with apricots or onions;
◆ Rue with basil, cabbage or sage;
◆ Sage with rue, wormwood or onions;
◆ Tomatoes with red cabbage, Brussels sprouts, sweetcorn, beetroot, dill or apricots; and
◆ Wormwood near compost as it repels earthworms.

Coriander produces its seeds on long, tall stems.

GROWING HERBS

BASIL

With its aromatic leaves, basil is one of the most popular culinary herbs. A frost-tender annual, it is easy to grow from seed or plant out bought seedlings. Basil, which grows to a height of about 40 cm, does best in a sunny spot in light, well-drained soil, with the plants 50 cm apart. Water regularly, especially in hot, dry weather. Pinch out tips and flowers to encourage leaf growth.

BAY

The bay is not a herbaceous plant but the spicy leaves are popular for flavouring food. It is a large but slow-growing evergreen tree which can eventually reach a height of 6 m with a spread of 2 m. It prefers a sunny position in rich, well-drained soil but will benefit from semi-shade in very hot areas. Water regularly while young and during long hot, dry spells once established. Bay trees make excellent container specimens because of their neat, compact growth. They can also be clipped into decorative shapes.

Quick-growing basil has many culinary uses.

Slow-growing evergreen bay makes a beautiful garden tree.

Neat rows of vegetables are surrounded by hedges of fragrant lavender.

Chervil

One of the few herbs which likes shade, chervil is happiest in well-prepared, moisture-retaining soil and where it gets only early morning sun. Chervil is an annual which grows readily from seed or seedlings. Plant each one about 20 cm apart and keep well watered. Nip off flowers to encourage leaf growth. It has a piquant taste, similar to parsley.

Chives

A clump-forming perennial of the onion family, chives can be grown from seed or you can plant out established plants. Chives do best in full sun and in fairly rich soil. Plant each one about 20 cm apart. Pick the outer leaves so that the plant always has enough foliage to encourage strong growth. The plant will die down in mid-summer under very hot conditions and also in mid-winter, but grows again rapidly when the conditions are more favourable.

The clumps should be divided every three to four years. Discard any very old or dried out fruitlets and only replant young, healthy ones. Common chives have blue-green, rounded stems and mauve flowers, while their close relative, garlic chives, has flat green stems and white flowers.

For the best results, do not allow garlic plants to flower.

As soon as flowers appear, nip them off the chervil plants.

Food from your Garden

As mints are very vigorous-growing plants, they must be kept under control.

Coriander

Grown for its sweet, spicy seeds, coriander is an easy-to-grow summer annual which prefers a good garden loam, full sun and protection from strong winds. Plant about 45 cm apart. A thick mulch will help keep the plant moist during hot weather. Pinch out coriander flowers to promote longer life.

Dill

A quick-growing summer annual, dill can be sown from seed or plant out established plants in well-drained, slightly acid soil. Dill needs plenty of sun but being a tall-growing plant (up to 75 cm) it should be protected from strong wind and well watered during dry weather. Pick dill flowers as soon as they are dry on the seedhead. The leaves are mildly spicy and the seeds pungent.

Fennel

An attractive, tall-growing perennial herb which grows up to 2 m, fennel has feathery green and purple foliage. Usually bought in plant form, it also grows easily from fresh seeds. Fennel likes a sunny to semi-shaded position and well-drained soil. It should be cut back hard after flowering. It self-seeds readily and can become a nuisance.

Garlic

Very similar to chives, garlic grows to about 60 cm. Garlic does best in partial shade and needs a well-drained soil. Flowers should be pinched out to encourage good clove formation. Cloves can be harvested once the foliage dies.

Mint

The various types of mint, including spearmint, peppermint, applemint and pennyroyal, are all strong growing perennials which like a rich, well-composted soil. They do best in semi-shade but will grow in full sun in cooler areas. Mint must always be kept well watered as dry conditions retard growth and spoil the quality of the leaves. As most are very vigorous growers, mints must be kept under control to stop them spreading too much and must be cut right down after flowering.

Parsley

Parsley is a biennial plant which flowers in its second year. Often treated as an annual, it can be grown quite easily from seed almost throughout the year or you can plant out established plants. Parsley does best in full sun or semi-shade in very hot areas. It likes a rich, well-drained soil and regular watering. Cutting off the flower heads and picking the leaves regularly will keep parsley growing well. Moss curled parsley is the most decorative and popular type but plain leaved parsley has a more pronounced flavour, especially in soups, stews and casseroles.

Fine foliaged dill has edible leaves and seeds.

Parsley lasts longer if not allowed to flower.

Herbs

Keep tarragon clipped back to encourage new growth.

Rosemary

An easy-to-grow, shrubby herb, rosemary does best in a light, well-drained, sandy soil and full sun. It needs an annual mulch of well-rotted manure. The upright rosemary grows to about 1 m high with a spread of about 45 cm, while the low-growing type has a height of about 60 cm and a spread of about 1,2 m. The plants should be trimmed to keep them bushy and full of new leaves, which have a pine-like fragrance.

Sage

Like mint, sage is perennial with a number of different types. It does best in a sunny to semi-shaded position in light, fertile, well-drained soil. Sage can be planted from a container at any time of the year or can be grown from cuttings done in spring or autumn but needs protection in cold, frosty areas. Once established, it should be pinched back regularly to encourage bushy growth. Use it to flavour savoury dishes.

Sweet Marjoram

A bushy perennial which does best in warm, frost-free areas, it can be planted from a container at any time of year or you can sow the seed in spring. It likes a sunny position in well-drained, fairly rich soil and must be well watered in hot weather. Cut off the flowers and clip back old stems to ensure plenty of new leaf growth. Use sweet marjoram to flavour savoury dishes. Common marjoram, better known as oregano, needs the same growing conditions as sweet marjoram. There are a number of other types of marjoram, for example, golden marjoram, which are grown mainly for their decorative foliage.

Tarragon

Also known as French tarragon, this perennial dies down in winter in cold areas. It needs a rich, well-drained, well-composted soil and a sunny position which is protected from strong winds. Seed is rarely available so tarragon is usually grown from divisions. It has a strong, aromatic taste and should be used sparingly when cooking. It makes an excellent herb vinegar.

Sweet marjoram is one of the most popular forms of this aromatic herb.

Rosemary makes an attractive and useful herb.

Food from your Garden

Thyme

With many different varieties to choose from, perennial thyme with its lemony flavour is one of the easiest herbs to grow but, like mint, some types of thyme can become quite invasive. Thyme does best in fertile, fairly light, well-drained soil in full sun. Keep the plants well watered, especially during long, dry spells. Clip back to keep neat and under control. Thyme can be propagated from seed, sown about 8-9 cm apart, or from cuttings made in spring or autumn.

When in flower, thyme makes a pretty display – faded flowers should be clipped off.

CONCENTRATED MINT SAUCE

fresh mint, enough to fill required number of jars

Finely chop up the mint and fill small glass jars with it until they are three-quarters full. Top up the jars with brown vinegar and cover with polythene or plastic-coated lids and store in the refrigerator.

To use, place mint in a bowl or sauce boat, add vinegar to form the desired consistency and add sugar to taste.

Note: The colour of the mint will darken with age but the flavour will remain good. It will keep for about three months in the fridge.

HERB VINEGAR

Put about 30 ml of a finely chopped, strong flavoured herb such as thyme, sage, chives and rosemary into a wide-necked jar. Add 500 ml warm brown vinegar. Cover with a glass or plastic lid and leave to infuse for two weeks. Remember to shake the jar occasionally.

Open the jar and taste the contents. If strong enough, strain through a fine sieve and pour into tall bottles. Put a fresh sprig of the herb into each bottle to identify it. If the flavour is not strong enough, leave for a little longer.
Makes about 1 bottle

PARSLEY BUTTER

100 g butter
10 ml chopped parsley
5 ml lemon juice
2,5 ml salt

Cream butter until soft, then add remaining ingredients. Make the butter into a roll about 2,5 cm thick. Wrap in wet greaseproof paper and leave to harden in the fridge.

BOUQUET GARNI

Bouquet garni is the name given to the small bunch of fresh or dried herbs which are used in many stocks, soups and casserole dishes. Vital ingredients include a bay leaf and 2 or 3 sprigs of leaves and stalks of parsley and thyme. Celery, crushed garlic and peppercorns can also be added.

When using fresh herbs, the little bunch (also known as a faggot) is tied together with a piece of string long enough to go around the handle of the saucepan so that it can easily be removed. With dried herbs, it is better to put them into a small muslin bag. This should also have a short string so that you can easily remove it from the pot.

GREEN MAYONNAISE

½ cup spinach leaves
1 cupful parsley sprigs
4 tarragon sprigs
4 chervil sprigs
300 ml mayonnaise
30 ml cream
salt
freshly ground black pepper

Wash and cook the spinach, parsley, tarragon and chervil in enough boiling salted water to cover until just tender. Drain thoroughly and press using a saucer until dry.

Push the pulp through a sieve. Stir the purée into the mayonnaise, stir in the cream and season with salt and pepper to taste. Chill before serving.

STORING HERBS

Freezing: Chop up the herbs you wish to freeze very finely. Fill ice cube trays with the various herbs, top up with water and then freeze. When you need the herbs for cooking, take out a cube and drop it into the dish during cooking. It will melt immediately and add a delicious flavour to the food.

Another method of freezing is to take sprigs of herbs and blanch them for half a minute in boiling water. Dry the herbs on absorbent kitchen paper and then store in very small freezer bags. When you want to use the herbs, just take out a bag, crumble up the frozen herbs and add to the dish.

Drying: Hang bundles of the small-leaved herbs, such as thyme and parsley, in a warm, dry, airy spot. Strip the leaves of the larger herbs and place them on a wire tray. Dry these herbs in your oven on the lowest setting with the oven door slightly open. A fan oven is particularly efficient for this. When the herbs are dry, crumble them up between your fingers and then store them in airtight jars for future use.

Herbs should be dried in a warm, dry, airy place.

COMFREY – THE GARDENER'S FRIEND

Comfrey is one of the many herbs with an extremely long history. Known in olden days as knitbone, comfrey leaves can be made into a poultice and used to heal bruises, swellings, strains and sprains, and the leaves can also be cooked.

It is its many uses that give comfrey pride of place in a food producing garden. With its deep, vigorous root system, comfrey is an extremely important companion plant as it brings up and retains vital trace elements which might not be so readily available to other plants. The leaves of comfrey, rich in all kinds of minerals and trace elements, can also be made into a highly beneficial liquid feed. Pack a large container, such as a garbage bin, half full with comfrey leaves and fill it up with water. Leave for about 3 weeks until the leaves have rotted down. Mix the comfrey water half and half with pure water and use to feed plants by watering it onto the soil around them. Comfrey leaves are also an excellent source of extra nutrients in the compost heap and help to decompose the organic materials more rapidly.

The tall-growing perennial comfrey is also useful in that it can provide some shade for other less heat tolerant plants. It prefers slightly acid soil and tends to die back in winter. Cut down as flowers begin to form so that the plant produces new growth.

A selection of frozen herbs ready for use.

Herbs frozen in ice blocks will provide you with just the right amount for use in savoury dishes year-round.

FREEZING YOUR PRODUCE

Freezing is the quickest and easiest method of storing your excess fruit, vegetables and herbs (*see* page 111) for use at a later date. It is important that you only use young vegetables and high quality, slightly unripe fruit for the best results.

UNDERSTANDING FREEZING METHODS

When foods are frozen, the liquid content of the food is turned into crystals. If frozen as quickly as possible or fast frozen, the crystals are small and the interior structure of the food is not adversely broken down when the food is cooked or defrosted. If allowed to freeze slowly, however, large crystals form within the cells and when these defrost, both the texture and the flavour of the food can be poor.

Most modern deepfreezes and freezer compartments of refrigerators will freeze food quickly. Over-large quantities should not be frozen all at once as this could cause a rise in temperature within the freezer which could affect the food already in it. As a general rule, fruit and vegetables take about one hour per 500 g to fast-freeze. Some freezers have a special fast-freeze setting which should be used if you would like to freeze very large quantities.

PACKAGING

While somewhat time-consuming, careful and correct packaging and preparation methods will ensure the best results. Many types of fruits and vegetables do not actually need wrapping, however, and can be frozen by the free-flow method and then packed into containers once frozen. Others will need to be blanched by immersing them in boiling water for a short time and then either frozen free-flow or packed into meal-sized units in freezer bags or boxes. While these are the two most widely used methods for freezing fruit and vegetables, fruit can also be frozen using the dry sugar pack method or the sugar syrup method.

FREE-FLOW FREEZING

Choose suitable types of fruit and vegetables (*see* page 115) which are in prime condition. Clean off any dirt but do not wash. If washing is unavoidable, dry as carefully and thoroughly as possible before freezing. Spread the items to be frozen on baking trays lined with greaseproof paper without letting them touch each other, and then freeze them uncovered. Once frozen, they can be repacked into freezer bags or boxes for easier storage; remember to repack just the right amount for one meal into each unit. While free-flow is an excellent method of freezing, the trays require plenty of space in the deep-freeze.

Blanching helps retain the colour and texture of certain vegetables.

F OOD FROM YOUR G ARDEN

HOW TO PREVENT FROSTING
To stop food from frosting while being frozen, you must ensure that all the air is removed from the packaging or container. Use a small suction pump to extract the air or use a straw which is just as efficient and less costly.

BLANCHING

To maintain the quality of some vegetables, they should be blanched in boiling water as this retards harmful enzyme action. Correct blanching also helps retain the colour and texture.

Put 500 g of the vegetable into a special blanching basket or a muslin bag. Bring 3,5 litres of water to boiling point in a large pot. Immerse the vegetables in the water for the required time (*see* chart on page 115), then cool as fast as possible by putting them into a bowl of iced water. When cool, drain on absorbent kitchen paper. The vegetables can then either be frozen free-flow or packed into boxes or freezer bags. When packing into bags or boxes, pack sufficient vegetables for one meal at a time. Use a suitable marking pen to label each one clearly.

Freeze portions of vegetables in sufficient amounts for your specific needs.

DRY SUGAR PACK

Some soft fruits, including pineapples and rhubarb, are best frozen by the dry sugar pack method. Place the dry, clean fruit on greaseproof paper. Measure out 100 g of sugar per 500 g of fruit. Sprinkle the fruit generously with the sugar and leave for several minutes until the juice begins to flow and forms a sugary syrup. Carefully roll the fruit in the syrup until thoroughly coated all over. The sugar aids preservation by drawing out some of the oxygen. Put into rigid boxes or containers with about 1 cm of head space above the fruit to allow for expansion, then freeze.

WHAT TO DO WITH DAMAGED FRUIT OR VEGETABLES
If you feel that your fruit or vegetables are not of a high enough quality to freeze whole or in segments, make them into a purée which can then be frozen. If you freeze vegetable purées in ice cube trays, you can take out as many as you need to make a vegetable stock to add to soups, stews and casseroles.

SUGAR SYRUP PACK

Soft fruit, especially deciduous stone fruits such as apricots and peaches, can be frozen by the sugar syrup method. Make a sugar syrup with 350 g of sugar and 600 ml of water. Bring to the boil, allow sugar to dissolve and then simmer for several minutes. Allow to cool before use. Clean the fruit and put onto suitable deep-sided trays or in shallow containers, then cover with 300 ml of syrup for every 500 g of fruit. Cover with a double layer of cellophane, seal leaving 1 cm of headspace to allow for expansion, and freeze. Label the containers clearly for easy identification.

Freezing Fruit

Fruit	Preparation	Method	Storage life
Apples	Peel, core, slice; blanch 1 minute	Free-flow	10 months
Apricots	Cut in half; remove stone	Sugar syrup	12 months
Berries	Under-ripe fruit	Free-flow	12 months
Citrus	Slice to use for drinks and decoration; grate peel	Free-flow	12 months
	Squeeze juice	Freeze juice	12 months
Melons	Cube or slice only	Sugar syrup	12 months
Peaches and nectarines	Use ripe, firm fruit; blanch 50 seconds; remove skin and stone	Sugar syrup	8 months
Pears	Skin and cut in half; poach for 2 minutes	Sugar syrup	12 months
Pineapple	Peel, cut into slices	Dry sugar	12 months
Rhubarb	Use tender stalks; cut into cubes	Dry sugar	12 months
Strawberries	Make into purée	Freeze	12 months

Freezing Vegetables

Vegetable	Preparation	Blanching time in minutes	Method	Storage in months
Beans – broad	Pod – use tender ones only	3	Pack in polythene bags	12
Beans – French	Trim ends – leave whole	2	Pack in polythene bags	12
Beetroot	Use small ones only; cook for 10-15 minutes, cool, slice or leave whole		Free-flow; pack in boxes	6
Broccoli	Divide into small sprigs, remove woody stalks	3	Free-flow; pack in boxes	12
Brussels sprouts	Use small, firm sprouts; trim outer leaves; make small cut in stem	3	Pack in polythene bags	12
Cabbage	Cut in wedges or shred – frozen cabbage cannot be used for salad	Wedges: 2 Shredded: 1	Pack in polythene bags	6
Carrots	Use small carrots; remove tops; rub off skin after blanching	4	Freeze in units, pack in bags	12
Cauliflower	Break into small florets; add lemon juice to blanching water	3	Freeze in units, pack in bags	9
Courgettes	Use small ones – leave whole or cut in slices	Whole: 2 Sliced: 1	Freeze in units, pack in bags	12
Parsnips and turnips	Same as for carrots			
Peas	Pod – use only tender ones	1	Free-flow, pack in bags	12
Spinach	Use unblemished leaves and stalks	2	Freeze in units, pack in bags	12
Tomatoes	Freeze whole or in halves		Free-flow, pack into bags	6

115

FRUIT AND VEGETABLE GARDENING CALENDAR

Correct timing in sowing, planting and general maintenance makes all the difference in the garden. Naturally this calendar may have to be adjusted to meet your area's climatic conditions but it should serve as a good, basic guide.

January

A number of deciduous fruits and vines will be ready for picking this month. Check their condition and pick while at their best. Never allow over-ripe fruit to lie on the ground as this encourages fruit fly. Collect fallen fruit, soak in water with a suitable insecticide and then bury or dispose of them along with household garbage – never put on a compost heap.

Trees and vines which have been harvested should be fed their second application of fertilizer (*see* individual entries).

Continue to spray late-bearing peaches against fruit fly and spray late apples and pears against codling moth.

Make sure that your fruit trees are kept well watered – at least every two to three weeks, depending on rainfall, and more often in dry summer conditions. Always soak trees thoroughly and keep well mulched.

Check citrus trees and thin out young fruit if necessary.

Summer vegetables should be watered regularly and the soil mulched. Weed by hand so as not to disturb crops. Apply a side-dressing of fertilizer or a liquid feed (*see* individual entries). Pick beans at least twice a week and spray tomatoes as a protective measure against early and late blight. *See* Vegetable Sowing Chart for vegetables which can be sown this month. Check the nurseries for the availability of young seedlings.

February

Always pick deciduous fruit regularly. Collect the fallen fruit and then fertilize deciduous trees which have finished bearing (*see* individual entries).

In order to destroy the last hatchings of fruit fly, use an appropriate fruit fly bait.

Once you have picked off the last of your granadillas, lightly prune back the plants to encourage new growth. Feed pawpaws and pineapples (*see* individual entries). Start to prepare beds for strawberries.

Keep late summer vegetables well watered and feed if necessary. Take out old crops which have finished producing – leaving them in encourages pests and diseases. Prepare empty beds and containers for new sowings and plantings.

Start transplanting winter seedlings such as broccoli, Brussels sprouts, cabbage and cauliflower as soon as they are big enough or when the plants are available from the nurseries. Continue to spray tomatoes against blight.

See Vegetable Sowing Chart on page 120 for vegetables which can be sown this month. Check nurseries for the availability of young seedlings. Be sure to choose cultivars which are best suited to your region's growing conditions.

Start gathering seeds of annual herbs such as dill, caraway, coriander, anise and fennel as soon as they ripen. Herbs which are flowering well, for example lavender, can be cut back and their flowers and foliage bunched and hung out to dry. Mulch the plants with compost.

March

The deciduous fruit season is drawing to a close. Feed the trees and vines once all the fruit has been harvested. Continue putting out fruit fly bait.

Most other fruit trees should be given their autumn application of fertilizer during this month. Always spread fertilizer evenly around the drip area and water in well. Water all trees, especially citrus, if weather is very hot and dry.

Young transplants of winter vegetables will benefit from light side-dressings of fertilizer or a liquid feed (*see* individual entries). Continue

Thin out citrus fruit if necessary. If not already done, prepare strawberry beds now.

Late summer vegetables must be kept well watered if quality of the crops is to be maintained. Keep the soil mulched and weed by hand.

to plant out transplants of winter vegetables depending on space and availability.

Spray tomatoes against fungal diseases. *See* Vegetable Sowing Chart for vegetables which can be sown this month. Check nurseries for availability of seedlings.

April

The deciduous fruit season is over but continue to put out fruit fly bait to try to destroy the last of these pests.

Keep citrus trees well watered and mulched – the first fruits should start to ripen at the end of the month, depending on climate and cultivars.

Feed guavas (*see* individual entry) and keep well watered in dry weather.

As late summer vegetables finish bearing, take them out and clean and prepare space for winter sowing. Feed young winter vegetables with a side-dressing of fertilizer or a liquid feed (*see* individual entries). Keep plants regularly watered, and keep weeding by hand so as not to disturb young plants.

See Vegetable Sowing Chart for seedlings which can be sown this month and check nurseries for the availability of seedlings.

May

Even though the main fruit season is over, keep putting out fruit fly bait as this pest can overwinter in evergreen shrubs and trees.

In summer rainfall regions, start pruning deciduous fruit trees and vines. All pruning cuts larger than a thick pencil should be sealed with sealing compound. After pruning, spray with fresh lime sulphur. Make sure the trees are thoroughly wetted and also spray the surrounding soil to kill off fungal spores which may be on the soil. Spray a second time after about 10 days.

In dry areas, water evergreens, especially citrus, every three to four weeks, but do not water mangoes which need to be kept dry before flowering. Keep the soil well-mulched with coarse compost. Remember that light, sandy soil will need water more frequently than heavy clay soils.

Watch winter vegetables such as Brussels sprouts, cauliflower and cabbages carefully for caterpillars and other pests. Help support peas by ridging up the soil around the stems and by putting in suitable pea sticks or bushy twigs.

June

Continue pruning fruit trees, vines and also berries in summer rainfall regions and start winter pruning in the winter rainfall areas. Seal larger cuts and spray with lime sulphur, with a second application after ten days.

In dry winter conditions, water evergreen fruit trees, except mangoes, and vines and berries about once a month. Check citrus trees, especially lemons and thin fruit if necessary.

Keep vegetables watered regularly and mulch the soil;

apply a side-dressing or a liquid feed to winter crops (see individual entries).

June is a poor sowing and planting month in most areas except parts of the winter rainfall regions and the subtropical areas.

July

Continue pruning and spraying deciduous fruit trees. Feed citrus after harvesting (see individual entry) as well as mangoes. Cut back granadillas to make them more bushy.

Continue routine care of winter vegetables. Take out plants which have been harvested – do not leave in cabbage or cauliflowers stalks as these can encourage pests and diseases. Start getting beds and containers ready for the new planting season.

See Vegetable Sowing Chart on page 120 for seed which can be sown this month and check nurseries for availability of young seedlings – where weather is favourable, try to get tomato transplants in as soon as possible for early crops.

August

Finish pruning deciduous fruit trees and vines. August marks one of the main fertilizing months for almost all fruit trees and vines (see individual entries).

Before feeding, lightly work old mulch into the soil, then water well and apply a new mulch. Keep watering all trees, vines, berries and strawberries in summer rainfall regions. Remove winter vegetables as soon as they are harvested and prepare soil thoroughly for the start of the new season. For early crops of vegetables which have a long initial growing period such as tomatoes, peppers and eggplants, as well as cucumbers and courgettes, sow seed in well-protected seed boxes.

Pests, especially snails, can wreak havoc on germinating seedlings so put down snail bait or use other preventative measures. If you have had any problems with cutworm on previous crops, work in cutworm bait to ensure even rows of vegetables.

See Vegetable Sowing Chart on page 120 for seed which can be sown this month and also check nurseries for the availability of young transplants, especially tomatoes.

September

With the start of spring comes the blossoming period of deciduous fruit trees. They will now need careful protection against fruit fly and codling moth. Begin your spraying routine as soon as the trees have reached the three-quarter petal drop stage (see individual entries). Start to thin out the tiny young fruit of apricots, peaches and plums (see individual entries).

Water fruit trees well if weather remains dry. Citrus needs to be watered about once a week as the flowers appear. Feed figs, pawpaws and strawberries (see individual entries).

Give close attention to newly sown seeds and young seedlings – water carefully every 3-4 days if weather is dry. Give first feed to young seedlings and transplants. Check and thin crops, such as carrots, if necessary. Spray tomatoes as a preventative against fungal diseases.

Take out the last of your winter crops; prepare the soil well for summer vegetables, according to variety. Always note where the old ones were growing so as to avoid planting the same crops in the same soil. Follow a crop rotation programme to stop the soil from being depleted of the same nutrients.

See Vegetable Sowing Chart for vegetables which can be sown this month and check the nurseries for the availability of transplants – try to get early transplants of tomatoes, peppers, eggplants and the various kinds of lettuce.

September is an excellent time to sow seed of various herbs, especially the annual herbs such as anise, basil, borage, chervil, coriander, dill, fennel, mustard and cress, and biennials like parsley. Your stock of herbs such as marjoram, thyme and mint can be increased by taking stem cuttings from established plants or softwood cuttings. Perennials such as fennel are easier to grow from seed.

October

Continue with spraying programme against fruit fly and codling moth on apples, pears, quinces, apricots, peaches and plums. Use bait instead of spray on trees where the fruit is almost ready for picking. Give trees a second thinning if necessary for bigger and better quality fruit.

Citrus must be well watered at this time if they are to produce good crops. Now is the time to prune back and feed guavas (*see* individual entry). Mangoes, pecans and litchis should also be fed. Strawberries should be starting to ripen – pick regularly and mulch well with compost.

Vegetables must be kept well watered as the weather gets warmer, especially if no rain has fallen. Water about every 3-4 days. Fruit fly can be a serious pest on all cucurbits so splash on fruit fly bait (*see* individual entries). Spray tomatoes against fungal diseases. Cucurbits may need protection against mildew.

See Vegetable Sowing Chart on page 120 for seed which can be sown during this month. There should be a number of young transplants available from the nurseries. Plant out young tomatoes, peppers and eggplants as soon as possible, especially in the cooler regions.

November

With plenty of deciduous fruit ripening now, protection against fruit fly and codling moth is important. Pick regularly and bury all fallen fruit.

Water fruit trees regularly, especially in dry weather. Make sure that cane berries such as boysenberries, loganberries, tayberries and youngberries get plenty of water. Pick fruit regularly. Heat-sensitive berries such as raspberries should also be kept very well mulched.

Summer vegetables will be coming on well. Keep the plants watered thoroughly in dry weather as sudden water stress spoils the quality. Mulch the soil between the plants to help keep them cool and retard weed growth.

Splash bait on cucurbits to protect them from pumpkin fly. Spray tomatoes against early and late blight and cucurbits against mildew. Make sure tomatoes are properly staked. *See* Vegetable Sowing Chart for vegetables which can be sown now and check your local nursery for the availability of young transplants. This is the main sowing period for broccoli, Brussels sprouts and cabbage and the beginning of the cauliflower sowing season.

Pinch out the flower heads of chervil to prevent the plants from flowering – this will prolong the season for being able to pick the leaves.

December

Spraying for fruit fly and codling moth must continue this month – if the trees are in full production, use a bait instead. Always remember to take careful note of withholding period when spraying the trees.

As soon as cane berries finish fruiting, cut the old fruiting canes back to ground level. As the new canes grow, tie them up to the supports. Give citrus a mid-season application of fertilizer. Remember to keep the trees well watered during the summer, particularly in dry summer areas. Put down thick layers of mulch to help keep the soil cool and damp. Use a very coarse compost.

Vegetables must be kept extremely well watered this month. Use plenty of mulch to help keep soil cool and damp. Keep picking beans two to three times a week to encourage more flower buds. Splash the leaves of cucurbits with bait to protect them against pumpkin fly.

Try to keep the foliage of tomatoes and cucurbits as dry as possible. Carefully surface irrigate the plants or, if overhead watering, apply water early in the day so that foliage is dry by nightfall.

See Vegetable Sowing Chart for vegetables which can be sown this month and check nurseries for the availability of transplants. This is still the main sowing season for broccoli, Brussels sprouts and cabbage, as well as cauliflower, in most areas.

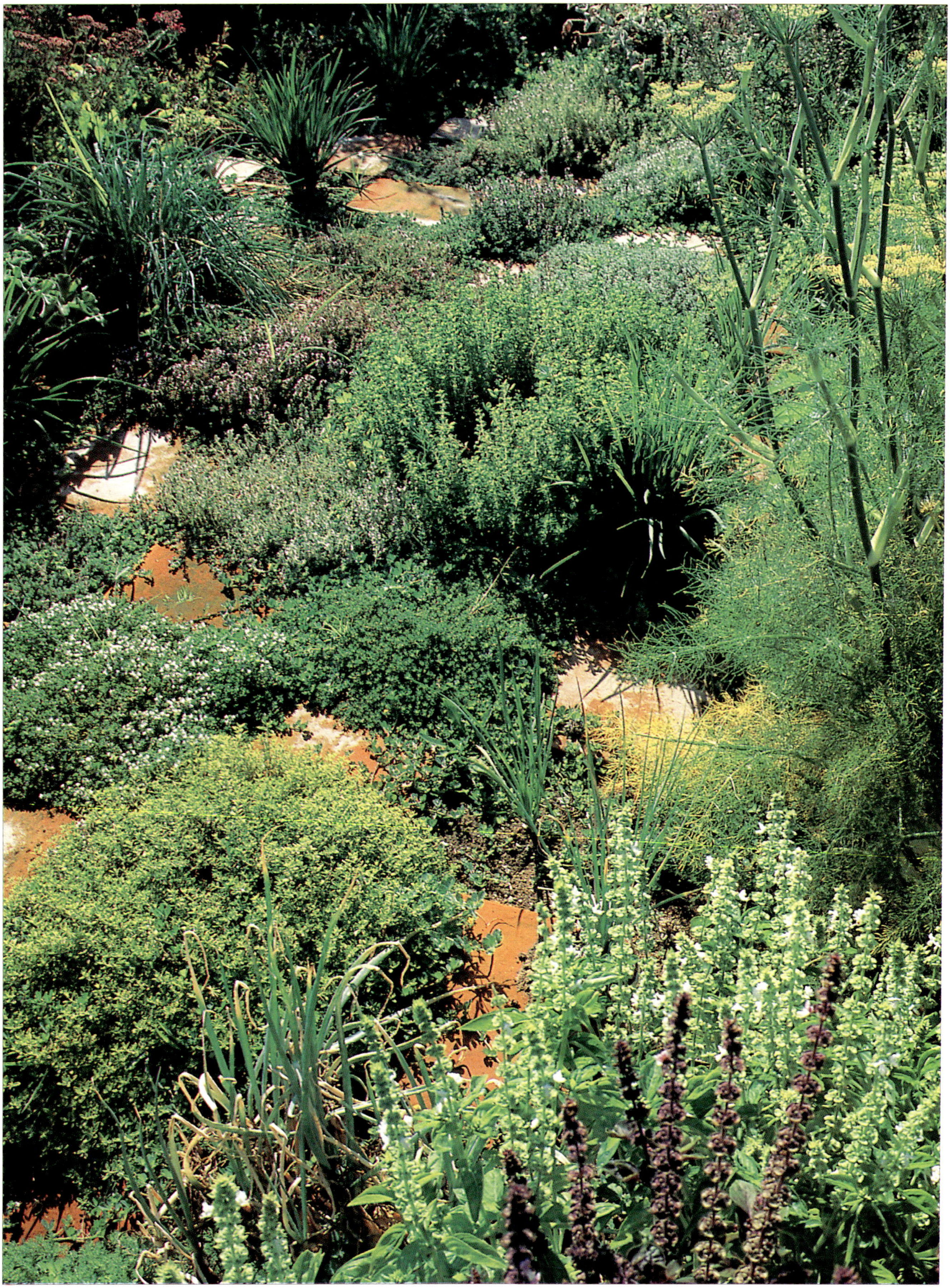

VEGETABLE SOWING CHART

1. Gauteng 2. Northern Transvaal and Eastern Transvaal 3. OFS, Northern Cape and Northwest Region 4. Natal Midlands 5. Eastern Cape 6. Western Cape 7. KwaZulu-Natal

VEGETABLE	REGION 1	2	3	4	5	6	7
Artichokes, globe	Jan	Jan-Feb	Jan	Jan	Jan	Jan	Jan-Feb
Artichokes, Jerusalem	Sep-Feb	Sep-Feb	Jul-Sep	Aug	Aug-Sep	Aug-Sep	Aug-Sep
Asparagus	Oct-Dec	Aug-Sep	Oct-Dec	Oct-Dec	Oct-Dec	Oct-Dec	Aug-Sep
Beans, broad	Apr-May	Apr-May	Apr	Apr-May	Apr-May	Apr-Jun	Apr-May
Beans, dwarf	Aug-Jan	Feb-Sep	Aug-Jan	Aug-Jan	Oct-Jan	Oct-Feb	Feb-Sep
Beans, runner	Aug-Dec	Feb-Aug	Aug-Dec	Aug-Dec	Oct-Dec	Sep-Jan	Feb-Aug
Beetroot	Aug-Oct Jan-Mar	Feb-Jul	Aug-Oct Feb-Mar	Aug-Apr	Jul-Feb	Jul-Nov Feb-Apr	Feb-Jul
Broccoli	Dec-Feb		Dec-Feb	Dec-Feb	Dec-Jan	Dec-Mar	
Brussels sprouts	Jan-Feb		Jan-Feb	Jan-Feb	Jan-Feb	Dec-Mar	
Cabbages	All year	Feb-Jun	Nov-Feb	All year	Aug-Apr	All year	Feb-Jun
Cabbages, Chinese	Feb-Mar		Feb-Mar	Feb-Mar	Feb-Mar	Feb-Mar	

Food from your Garden

Carrots	All year	Feb-Aug	Aug-Oct Jan-Mar	All year	Jul-Apr	All year	Feb-Aug
Cauliflowers (early)	Nov-Dec		Nov-Dec	Dec-Feb	Dec-Jan	Nov-Dec	
Cauliflowers (main crop)	Dec-Feb	Feb-Mar	Nov-Feb	Dec-Mar	Dec-Mar	Dec-Jan	Feb-Mar
Cauliflowers (late)	Mar				Mar-Apr	Feb-Apr	
Celery	Sep-Dec	Feb-Mar	Sep-Oct	Feb-Mar Aug-Sep	Feb-Mar Aug-Sep	Feb-Oct	Feb-Mar
Cucumbers	Sep-Dec	Feb-Sep	Sep-Dec	Sep-Dec	Jul-Feb	Sep-Nov	Feb-Sep
Eggplants	Aug-Oct	Jan-Sep	Aug-Oct	Aug-Oct	Aug-Oct	Aug-Oct	Jan-Sep
Kohlrabi	Jan-Mar	Mar-May	Jan-Mar	Feb-May	Jan-Mar	Jan-Mar	Mar-May
Leeks	Jan-Mar	Mar-Apr	Jan-Feb	Feb-Mar	Feb-Apr	Mar-May	Mar-Apr
Lettuce	All year	Mar-May	Jan-Mar Aug-Sep	All year	Jan-Apr Jul-Oct	All year	Mar-May
Melons, sweet	Sep-Nov	Jun-Aug	Sep-Oct		Sep-Oct	Sep-Dec	Jun-Aug
Onions	Feb-Mar	Feb-Mar	Mar-Jul	Feb-Mar	Mar-May	Apr-May	Feb-Mar
Parsnips	Aug-Oct Jan-Mar	Mar-Apr	Jan-Mar	Jul-Sep Jan-Apr	Aug-Oct Feb-Apr	Mar-Apr Aug-Oct	Mar-Apr

Vegetable Sowing Chart

Peas	Jul-Sep Mar	Mar-Jun	Jul-Aug	Jun-Jul Mar	May-Jul	Apr-Aug	Mar-Jun
Peppers	Aug-Oct	Jan-Apr Jul-Oct	Aug-Oct	Sep-Oct	Aug-Oct	Aug-Oct	Jan-Apr Jul-Oct
Potatoes (see page 80)							
Pumpkins and hubbard squash	Sep-Nov	Feb-Aug	Sep-Dec	Sep-Dec	Sep-Nov	Sep-Nov	Feb-Aug
Radishes	Aug-Nov Feb-Apr	Feb-Sep	Aug-Oct Feb-Mar	Aug-Oct Jan-Apr	Aug-May	Mar-Oct	Feb-Sep
Rhubarb	Aug-Sep	Mar-Apr	Aug-Sep	Aug-Sep	Aug-Oct	Aug-Sep	Mar-Apr
Spinach	Aug-Apr	Feb-Jun	Aug-Apr	Aug-Apr	Aug-Sep	Mar-May	Feb-Jun
Squashes	Sep-Nov	Feb-Aug	Aug-Nov	Sep-Nov	Sep-Dec	Aug-Jan	Feb-Aug
Sweetcorn	Sep-Nov	Jul-Nov	Aug-Nov	Sep-Nov	Sep-Dec	Aug-Dec	Jul-Nov
Sweet potatoes	Oct-Dec	Oct-Dec	Oct-Jan	Oct-Dec	Oct-Dec	Aug-Dec	Oct-Nov
Swiss chard	Aug-Oct Jan-Mar	Feb-Aug	Jan-Mar Jul-Oct	Aug-Oct Jan-Mar	Aug-Oct Jan-Mar	Mar-Apr Aug-Sep	Feb-Aug
Tomatoes	Aug-Nov	Jan-Jul	Aug-Nov	Aug-Nov	Aug-Oct	Jul-Sep	Jan-Jul
Turnips	Aug-Sep Jan-Apr	Feb-Jun	Aug-Sep Jan-Apr	Jan-Apr Aug-Sep	Jul-Aug Feb-Mar	Mar-Nov	Feb-Jun

GLOSSARY

Acid soil Soil with a pH level below 7,0; a slightly acid soil is preferred by most fruit and vegetables

Aeration The loosening of the soil by various mechanical means to allow free passage of air

Alkaline soil Soil with a pH of above 7

Annual Plants grown from seed which mature within a year

Aubergine Eggplant

Bare-rooted Applies to deciduous fruit trees, vines and cane fruits which are dug out in winter, have the soil removed from their roots, are then wrapped in hessian sacking and sold for replanting

Biennial Plants maturing in the second year after planting

Biodegradable Materials readily decomposed in the soil by micro-organisms such as bacteria

Blanching Excluding light from the stems and leaves of vegetables, such as celery, to whiten and improve the flavour and texture

Bolting Premature running to seed, often as a result of excessive heat, drought or poor soil; cauliflower, cabbage and lettuce are prone to bolting

Brassica Members of the cabbage family: broccoli, Brussels sprouts, cabbage, cauliflower and kale

Brinjal Eggplant

Broadcast A method of sowing seed or spreading fertilizer by spreading evenly over a large area but not in rows

Bud burst The opening of buds of deciduous species in spring

Bud drop The dropping off of the flower buds of fruit trees and the failure to set fruit; due mainly to adverse weather, drought or poor nutrition

Cane Slender woody stem, often pithy in the centre; loganberries, youngberries and tayberries are typical canes; also known as cane fruit

Chlorosis Lack of green colouring in the leaves, giving bleached, yellow appearance; mainly caused by lack of essential minerals

Complete fertilizer A fertilizer mixture which contains nitrogen, phophate and potassium; also called balanced fertilizer

Cross-pollination The transfer of pollen from the flowers of one fruit tree to another of the same type, essential in a number of deciduous fruits

Cruciferae Extension of the brassica family to include radish, turnip, kohlrabi and swedes

Cucurbit The squash family: marrows, melons, cucumbers and pumpkins

Cultivar A variety of plant specifically bred and cultivated by man, known as a CULTIvated VARiety or cultivar

Curd The tightly packed, immature flower heads on cauliflowers and broccoli

Damping off A fungal disease which causes seedlings to die either just before or after they have emerged

Defoliation Unnatural loss of foliage by a tree due to wind, heat, drought, pests or diseases

Determinate A plant which stops growing from the main stem once the terminal buds form flowers, e.g. certain tomato cultivars

Die-back The dying back of a stem from the apex due to disease, drought or excess water and poor drainage

Double digging A method of digging the soil to two spades depth, usually putting the top spadeful of topsoil to one side and the second spade of subsoil on the other side, often associated with the digging of vegetable trenches

Drift The spray emitted from sprayers, often a fine, high-pressure spray, which, in the case of weedkillers, can damage nearby plants

Drill A straight, very shallow furrow in the soil into which seed is sown

Drip line The circle beneath a tree's outer branches where the heaviest drip occurs when it rains; this is where the trees roots are the most active and where fertilizers should be applied

Earth-up To heap soil up and around the stems of plants, such as celery and leeks, to keep them white or to protect from sunlight, such potatoes

Fallow Soil which is left unplanted after a crop has been removed

F1 Hybrid Plants of a first generation hybrid of two dissimilar plants

Foliar feed To fertilize plants by using a liquid which is absorbed through the plants leaves

Friable Soil which is crumbly and easy to cultivate

Harden off To gradually move plants, usually seedlings, from a sheltered position, for example, in a greenhouse into the open garden

Hardy A plant which is able to tolerate severe frost without suffering damage

Glossary

Hard-pan The almost impenetrable layer of soil situated below the topsoil, usually caused by continuously cultivating the soil to that same depth

Heading back The cutting back of the main stem (leader) or side stems (laterals) to encourage compact growth, mainly associated with deciduous fruit trees, such as pears

Heavy soil Soils which are hard to work, often clay soil, which in olden days needed to be ploughed by a team of heavy horses

Hilling-up The banking up of soil around the stem of a plant to give it extra support

Honeydew The sticky excretia of scale insects which attracts ants and various other insects

Indeterminate A plant which will go on growing until stopped as it has no true terminal point; associated with certain tomato cultivars

Intercrop To grow quick-maturing plants, especially vegetables, between slower types to make maximum use of the available space

Lateral The shoot or stem which arises from the leaf axis of a larger stem; associated with deciduous fruit trees

Leaching The washing out of soluble soil nutrients by water

Leader A central upward shoot of a tree

Mulch A layer of decomposed organic matter used to conserve soil moisture

Nematodes Minute roundworms, many species of which are plant parasitic

Neutral soil A soil with a pH of 7,0

Nitrogen fixation The changing of nitrogen in the air into nitrogen which can be used by plants through the nitrification of bacteria found on the roots of legumes

Overwinter Pests are protected by bark and leaves of a tree during winter

Perennial Plants which live for a number of years and do not die after flowering and seeding

Pinching back The nipping off of the main growing point of a plant to encourage side growth

Potting-on The transplanting of plants from a small container into a large one

Pre-planting fertilizer A fertilizer which is worked into the soil before planting, for example, 2.3.2

Pricking out The transplanting of seedlings from seed boxes or seed beds into other seed trays or into the ground

Ridging The drawing up of soil along the base of the plant, for example, potatoes, to protect the tubers which are just at the surface

Semi-hardy A plant which will tolerate only moderate frost without damage

Side-dressing An application of fertilizer which is close to the plant at soil level, usually given to young vegetable plants

Soil conditioner Material used to improve fertility and texture of soil, often associated with concentrated organic materials

Spit A measurement approximately 25 cm, or the depth of the blade of an average garden spade or fork

Spur A compact shoot containing both wood and fruit buds, usually associated with deciduous fruit trees such as apples and pears

Stopping The breaking off or pinching out of a growth bud to encourage bush growth or flower set

Strain A particular selection of a variety or species raised from seed, associated with annuals

Systemic Refers to pesticides, fungicides or herbicides which are absorbed through foliage into a plants sap system, making the sap toxic to pests

Tender Any plant which cannot tolerate frost

Thinning out The removing of individual seedlings within a planting to give the remaining ones sufficient space to develop; the removal of branches from trees to allow in more sun and air; the removal of very immature fruits to allow space for the remainder to develop to a larger size

Tilth The fine, crumbly top layer of soil produced by digging and raking, associated with the preparation of soil for seed sowing

Trench Refers to the deep digging of strips of soil, up to 1 m deep, associated with the preparation of vegetable beds

True leaf The leaf which develops after a seed produces the seed leaf or first leaf

Tuber A thick, fleshy underground stem which stores starch as a reserve of food material for the plant

Variety A sub-division, often naturally occurring, of a plant species (*see entry under Cultivar*)

Vine crops Plants which trail or spread along the ground, for example, melons and squashes

Water stress The condition of plants which are unable to absorb water lost through transpiration, resulting in wilting, growth halt and even death

Wilting point The point when there is not enough soil moisture to meet the needs of a plant

Withholding period The period between the last application of an insecticide or fungicide and the breakdown of their residues when it becomes safe to eat the crops that have been sprayed, especially with vegetables

INDEX

A
almonds 100
alternaria 28
American bollworm 25
anthracnose 28
aphids 25
apples 79, 100, 104
apricots 79, 81
　at a glance 81
　growing apricots 81
　possible problems 82
　recommended cultivars 82
artificial fertilizers 16, 17
astylus beetle 25
Australian bug 27
avocado 79, 100

B
bad companions 106
bananas 79, 100
basil 104, 106
bay 106
beans 38, 44, 45, 48, 104
　at a glance 49
　growing beans 48
　possible problems 49
　recommended cultivars 49
　types 48
beetroot 38, 44, 45, 50, 104
　at a glance 50
　growing beetroot 50
　possible problems 50
　recommended cultivars 50
beneficial insects 28-30
　hover flies 30
　lacewings 30
　ladybirds 30
　praying mantis 30
　spiders 30
　wasps 30
berries 79, 82
　at a glance 83
　cottage cheese with berries 82
　growing berries 82
　possible problems 83
blanching 114
borage 104
boysenberries 79
broad beans 75
broccoli 38, 44, 45, 51, 104
　at a glance 51
　growing broccoli 51
　possible problems 51
　recommended cultivar 51
Brussels sprouts 44, 45, 75

C
cabbage 38, 52, 104
　at a glance 52
　growing cabbage 52
　possible problems 53
　recommended cultivars 53
　salad 53
　types of cabbage 52
calendar, fruit and vegetable 116
Cape gooseberry 101
carrots 38, 44, 45, 54, 104
　at a glance 54
　growing carrots 54
　possible problems 54
　recommended cultivars 54
cauliflower 44, 45, 55
　at a glance 56
　cauliflower cheese 56
　growing cauliflower 55
　possible problems 55
　recommended cultivars 55
celery 44, 45, 75, 104
chemical products
　do's and don'ts 31
　using 30
cherries 79
cherry guavas 101
chervil 104, 107
Chinese cabbage 44, 45
chives 104, 107
citrus 79, 84
　at a glance 85
　growing citrus 84
　possible problems 85
　recommended cultivars 85
　three fruit marmalade 86
　types of citrus 84
climate
　and plant growth 13
　guide 45, 79
CMR beetle 27
comfrey 111
companion plants 11
　bad companions 106
　good companions 104
　what is companion planting? 103
compost
　do's and don'ts 19
　how to add to the soil 22
　how to make 19
　or fertilizers? 18
containers 37
　container candidates 38
　container care 39

container choice 37
potatoes in containers 39
replanting containers 39
soil and drainage 38
what to grow 38
which vegetables to choose 38
control measures 31
coriander 108
courgettes 44, 45, 56
　at a glance 57
　growing courgettes 56
　possible problems 57
　recommended cultivars 57
crop rotation 47
cucumbers 38, 44, 58
　at a glance 59
　growing cucumbers 58
　iced cucumber soup 59
　possible problems 59
　recommended cultivars 59
cultivars 46, 80
cutworm 27

D
damping off 28
diamond-back moth caterpillar 27
dill 104, 108
downy mildew 29
dry sugar pack 114

E
eggplant 38, 45, 104

F
fennel 108
fertilizers
　artificial 16, 17
　how to apply to growing plants 20
　how to apply to new beds 20
　how to apply to trees 21
　liquid fertilizer, how to apply 21
　or compost? 18
　organic fertilizers and manures 17
　pre-planting fertilizer 20
　side-dressing fertilizer 20
figs 79, 87
　at a glance 87
　growing figs 87
　possible problems 87
　recommended cultivars 87
freezing your produce 113

freezing fruit 115
freezing methods 113
　blanching 114
　dry sugar pack 114
　free-flow freezing 113
　packaging 113
　prevent frosting 114
　sugar syrup pack 114
freezing vegetables 115
what to do with damaged fruit or vegetables 114
fruit 79
　almonds 100
　apples 79, 100, 104
　apricots 79, 81
　avocado 79, 100
　bananas 79, 100
　berries 79, 82
　bought plants or home-grown? 80
　boysenberries 79
　Cape gooseberry 101
　cherries 79
　cherry guavas 101
　citrus 79, 84
　climate guide 79
　cold climate fruit 79
　cultivars 80
　figs 79, 87
　granadillas 79, 88
　grapes 79, 89, 104
　guavas 79, 92
　Kiwi fruit 100
　litchis 79, 100
　macadamia nuts 79, 100
　mangoes 79, 100
　pawpaws 79, 93
　peaches and nectarines 95
　pears 79, 101
　pecan nuts 79, 101
　persimmons 79, 101
　pick of the crop 80
　pineapple guavas 101
　plums 79, 97
　prolific producers 79
　quinces 79, 101
　raspberries 79
　strawberries 79, 98, 104
　subtropical climate fruit 79
　temperate climate fruit 79
　tree tomatoes 79, 101
　trees to be avoided 80
　where to plant 79
fruit and vegetable gardening calendar 116

126

Index

fruit fly 27
fruit trees
  where to plant 10
  and garden design 10
fruiting vines and creepers,
where to plant 10
fungal diseases 28
  alternaria 28
  anthracnose 28
  damping off 28
  downy milew 29
  late blight 29
  powdery mildew 29
  rust 29

G
garlic 104, 108
garlic spray 31
glossary 124
gooseberry, Cape 101
granadillas 79, 88
  at a glance 88
  growing granadillas 88
  possible problems 88
grapes 79, 89, 104
  at a glance 90
  green grape mould 91
  growing grapes 89
  possible problems 91
  recommended cultivars 91
greater cabbage moth caterpillar 27
green shield bugs 27
grow bag 37
guavas 79, 92
  at a glance 92
  growing guavas 92
  possible problems 92
  recommended cultivars 92

H
herbal spray 31
herbs 103
  and companion plants 11, 103
  and good companions 104
  bad companions 106
  basil 104, 106
  bay 106
  bouquet garni 110
  chervil 104, 107
  chives 104, 107
  comfrey 111
  coriander 108
  dill 104, 108
  fennel 108
  garlic 104, 108
  growing herbs 106
  herb vinegar 110
  mayonnaise, green 110
  mint 104, 108
  mint sauce 110
  parsley 108
  parsley butter 110
  rosemary 104, 109
  sage 104, 109
  storing herbs 111
  sweet marjoram 109
  tarragon 109
  thyme 104, 110
home-made sprays 31
hover flies 30
how to ... 19
  add compost to the soil 22
  apply granular fertilizers
    to growing plants 20
    to new beds 20
    to trees 21
  avoid problems 30
  change pH levels 20
  control weeds 24
  make compost 19
  mulch 22
  plant a strawberry barrel 37
  plant trees and shrubs 19
  prepare vegetable beds 19
  raise vegetable seedlings 22
  sow vegetable seeds in a furrow 22
  stake tomatoes 73
  transplant seedlings 22
  use liquid fertilizer 21
  use waste water 24
  use water effectively 24

K
kale 44, 45
Kiwi fruit 100
kohlrabi 45

L
lacewings 30
ladybirds 30
late blight 29
leeks 45, 60, 104
  at a glance 60
  growing leeks 60
  helpful hints 60
  possible problems 60
  recommended cultivars 60
lettuce 38, 44, 45, 61, 104
  at a glance 62
  growing lettuces 61
  possible problems 62
  recommended cultivars 62
  types of lettuce 61
litchis 79, 100

M
macadamia nuts 79, 100
mangoes 79, 100
manure, organic 17
marrows 45
mealie bug 27
mealies 45
melons 45
mint 104, 108
mulch, how to 22

O
onions 45, 75
organic gardening, what is it? 18
organic fertilizers and manures 17

P
packaging 113
parsley 108
parsnips 44, 45, 76
pawpaws 79, 93
  at a glance 94
  growing pawpaws 93
  pawpaw as a tenderizer 94
  possible problems 94
peaches and nectarines 79, 95
  at a glance 96
  brandied peaches 94
  growing peaches and nectarines 95
  possible problems 96
  recommended cultivars 96
pears 79, 101
pear slug 27
peas 39, 44, 45, 63
  at a glance 64
  growing peas 63
  possible problems 64
  recommended cultivars 64
  types of peas 63
pecan nuts 79, 101
peppers 39, 45, 65
  at a glance 66
  growing peppers 65
  possible problems 66
  recommended cultivars 66
  types of pepper 65
  vegetarian stuffed peppers 66
pernicious scale 27
persimmons 79, 101
pests, diseases and disorders 25
  American bollworm 25
  aphids 25
  astylus beetle 25
  Australian bug 27
  CMR beetle 27
  cutworm 27
  diamond-back moth caterpillar 27
  fruit fly 27
  greater cabbage moth caterpillar 27
  green shield bugs 27
  mealie bug 27
  pear slug 27
  pernicious scale 27
  plusia looper caterpillar 27
  red spider mite 27
  scale 27
  slugs and snails 27
  stink bugs 28
  thrips 28
  white fly 28
pH levels
  how to change 20
  role 15
pineapple guavas 101
planning for success 8
plant them in pots 37
plums 79, 97
  at a glance 97
  growing plums 97
  plum and apple jam 98
  possible problems 97
  recommended cultivars 98
plusia looper caterpillar 27
potatoes 39, 45, 66, 104
  at a glance 67
  growing potatoes 66
  in containers 39
  possible problems 68
  potato salad 68
  recommended cultivars 68
potting soil recipe 38
powdery mildew 29
praying mantis 30
pruning 33
  hints 35
  methods 33
    central leader method 33
    modified natural shape 34
    pinching out 35
    pruning vines over a pergola 34
    summer pruning 34
    thinning fruit 35
    vase shape 33
pumpkin 44, 45

Q
quinces 79, 101

R
radishes 39, 44, 45, 76, 104
raspberries 79
recipes
  bouquet garni 110
  brandied peaches 94
  cabbage salad 53
  cauliflower cheese 56
  concentrated mint sauce 110
  cottage cheese with berries 82
  green grape mould 91
  green mayonnaise 110
  herb vinegar 110

iced cucumber soup 59
parsley butter 110
pawpaw as a tenderizer 94
plum and apple jam 98
potato salad 68
spinach soufflé 70
stuffed hubbard squash 77
three fruit marmalade 86
vegetarian stuffed peppers 66
red spider mite 27
rosemary 104, 109
rust 29

S
sage 104, 109
scale 27
seedlings
  how to transplant 22
  or seed 47
  vegetable seedlings, how to raise 22
shrubs, how to plant 19
slugs and snails 27
soap spray 31
soil
  and drainage in containers 38
  and plant growth 13
  how to improve your soil 15
  potting soil recipe 38
  what kind do you have? 15
sowing chart, vegetable 120
spiders 30
spinach 39, 44, 45, 76
  Swiss chard 39, 44, 45, 69
sprays, home-made 31
  garlic spray 31
  herbal spray 31
  soap spray 31
squash 44, 45, 76

stuffed hubbard squash 77
stink bugs 28
strawberries 79, 98, 104
  at a glance 99
  growing strawberries 98
  possible problems 99
  recommended cultivars 99
  strawberry barrel, how to plant 37
sugar syrup pack 114
swedes 44
sweetcorn 44, 45, 77, 104
sweet marjoram 109
sweet melons 77
sweet potatoes 45
Swiss chard spinach 44, 45, 69
  at a glance 69
  growing Swiss chard spinach 69
  possible problems 70
  recommended cultivars 70
  spinach soufflé 70

T
tarragon 109
thrips 28
thyme 104, 110
tomatoes 39, 44, 45, 71, 104
  at a glance 72
  growing tomatoes 71
  how to stake tomatoes 73
  possible problems 72
  recommended cultivars 73
  types of tomatoes 71
trees, how to plant 19
tree tomatoes 79, 101
turnips 39, 44, 74
  at a glance 74
  growing turnips 74

possible problems 74
recommended cultivars 74

V
vegetable beds
  how many? 41
  how to prepare 19
  preparing the ground 43
  size and shape 41
vegetables 41
  beans 38, 44, 45, 48, 104
  beetroot 38, 44, 45, 50, 104
  broad beans 75
  broccoli 38, 44, 45, 51, 104
  Brussels sprouts 44, 45, 75
  cabbage 38, 44, 45, 52, 104
  carrots 38, 44, 45, 54, 104
  cauliflower 44, 45, 55
  celery 44, 45, 75, 104
  cool season 45
  courgettes 44, 45, 56
  crop rotation 47
  cucumbers 38, 44, 58
  cultivars 46
  eggplant 38, 45, 104
  feast or famine 46
  for your freezer 44
  high yields, small space 44
  intermediate 45
  kale 44, 45
  kohlrabi 45
  leeks 45, 60, 104
  lettuce 38, 44, 45, 61, 104
  onions 45, 75
  parsnips 44, 45, 76
  peas 39, 44, 45, 63
  peppers 39, 45, 65
  planning tips 46
  planting distances 46

potatoes 39, 45, 66, 104
radishes 44, 45, 76
seedlings, how to raise 22
seed or seedlings 47
seeds, how to sow in a furrow 22
sowing chart 120
spinach 39, 44, 45, 76
squash 44, 45, 76
summer and winter vegetables 41
sweet melons 77
sweetcorn 44, 45, 77
Swiss chard spinach 39, 44, 45, 69
tomatoes 3, 44, 45, 71, 104
turnips 39, 44, 74
warm season 45
what to grow 43
when to plant 45
where to plant 9
vines, how to prune 34

W
walnuts 79
wasps 30
water
  how to use effectively 24
  waste water, how to use 24
weeds, how to control 24
what makes plants grow? 13
white fly 28
where to plant
  fruit trees 10
  fruiting vines and creepers 10
  vegetables 9

Y
youngberries 79